ALEXANDER HAMILTON

HOW THE MIGHTY ARE REDEEMED

CHRISTOPHER S. YATES

ALEXANDER HAMILTON: HOW THE MIGHTY ARE REDEEMED
By Christopher S. Yates
© 2000 by the Family Research Council

Family Research Council
801 G Street, NW
Washington, DC 20001
(800) 225-4008
www.frc.org

ISBN 1-55872-006-5
Library of Congress Card Number 00-108269

In Memory of

THE HONORABLE WILLIAM E. SIMON

U.S. Secretary of the Treasury

May 8, 1974, to January 20, 1977

They, forthwith to the place
Repairing where he judged them, prostrate fell
Before him reverent, and both confessed
Humbly their faults, and pardon begged, with tears
Wat'ring the ground, and with their sighs the air
Frequenting, sent from hearts contrite, in sign
Of sorrow unfeigned and humiliation meek.

Thus they, in lowliest plight, repentant stood
Praying; from the mercy-seat above
Prevenient grace descending had removed
The stony from their hearts, and made new flesh
Regenerate grow instead, that sighs now breathed
Unutterable, which the Spirit of prayer
Inspired, and winged for Heaven with speedier flight
Than loudest oratory.

John Milton
Paradise Lost, Books 10 and 11

CONTENTS

PREFACE

G. K. Chesterton once opined, "Original sin is the one Christian doctrine proved by four thousand years of recorded history." Likewise, when a fellow journalist asked, "What's wrong with the world?" Chesterton quipped, "I am." As an observer of culture, society, and events, Chesterton was convinced that the human race is a fallen one. Not the only thinker to wrestle with the plight of humanity, he can be counted with the biblical prophets and poets, ancient Greek and Roman philosophers, St. Augustine and St. Thomas, John Calvin and Jonathan Edwards, and my friend Michael Cromartie. Cromartie, a vice president at the Ethics and Public Policy Center, often says, "As a conservative I believe in virtue and vice, but more in vice."

The human paradox is that men and women are creatures capable of great deeds of dignity as well as horrific depths of depravity. Attempting to explain this reality has been the work of theologians and philosophers through the ages. In the biblical narrative and in subsequent Christian thought down to the present day, this paradoxical condition is explained by the Fall. Humankind was created good and beautiful, but because of moral rebellion, it is now broken. The idea of original sin or the Fall, however, does not mean that the personal, social, and moral predicament is as bad as it possibly can be. Rather, in the words of the *Common Prayer Book* used by Alexander Hamilton, humanity is "very far gone" from original righteousness. Whatever goodness and beauty remains in the essence of human nature is tarred and tarnished. Like Adam and Eve in Milton's *Paradise Lost*, all men and women are in desperate need of redemption and regeneration.

If, as Plato observed, the *polis* (city) is the soul writ at large, then politics is the extension of the human soul. Basic ideas about human nature are therefore crucial to political assumptions and actions necessary to public life and liberty. Fallenness is one of those ideas. The fallenness of humanity is a fundament of life and therefore of public life.

Alexander Hamilton: How the Mighty Are Redeemed is an inspiring and compelling story about human fallenness and redemption. Its bright and promising young author, Christopher S. Yates, began writing this story while a Witherspoon Fellow at the Family Research Council in the fall of 1999. Shortly after beginning the project, Christopher (having had the opportunity to study both men) observed, "Alexander Hamilton is not John Witherspoon." Witherspoon is a largely forgotten American founder who nevertheless looms large on the horizon of the American republic. A signer of the Declaration of Independence as well as a teacher and mentor to a generation of American leaders, including James Madison, his public figure was larger than life. As a well educated clergyman, moral philosopher, college president, and citizen-patriot, his public reputation and honor were above reproach, and his contribution to nation-building was substantial. Witherspoon may have been the most consistently Christian of the American founders. Profoundly motivated by religious and theological commitments that proved a north star in his public and private life, he was a man whose closet contained no skeletons. Hamilton is a different story.

Alexander Hamilton began his life in the Caribbean Islands as an illegitimate child but went on to make a name for himself as an American patriot, soldier, author, and cabinet member. Yet amid the dirty politics of the 1790s, Hamilton was caught in an embarrassing public scandal involving a tawdry sexual affair and political hush money. In 1801, he was struck a hard blow when his eldest son, Philip, was killed. To make matters worse, Philip's death drove Hamilton's oldest daughter to permanent insanity.

Recoiling from the heartache of family problems, Hamilton continued to occupy himself with national and international affairs even after his political career ended. The French Revolution had become a bloodbath of atheism; Hamilton believed that its ideologies presented a clear and present danger to the fledgling American republic. Robespierre's Reign of Terror and Napoleon's dictatorship prompted Hamilton to more serious reflection about the religious and moral foundation of republican political order, particularly concerning the relationship of Christianity to the American Constitution. By 1802, Hamilton expressed grave doubts about the surety of the United States' religious and moral underpinnings. In response, Hamilton proposed the formation of what, in retrospect, looks like a lobbying group not unlike some organizations of religious conservatives today. Its mission was to propagate the Christian faith and to support the constitutional order. The idea, however, never materialized. Hamilton was shot and mortally wounded in a duel with Aaron Burr Jr. in 1804.

The last four years of Hamilton's life particularly interest students of religion and politics. During this time, Hamilton's private and public worlds were imploding. The pressing issues of family tragedy, public shame, political misfortune, and the international ideologies of modernism appear to have driven him to his knees. The once high and mighty Hamilton now took a posture of penitence. Fallen, wayward, and sinful, Hamilton wanted regeneration, repair, and restoration. Thus, on his deathbed "in lowliest plight," Hamilton sought the grace and mercy of God.

Mr. Yates recounts the captivating drama of Hamilton's redemption, which not only instructs but also inspires those of us who would like to learn more about what C. S. Lewis calls the "first things" of God, particularly as they bear on "second things" of civilization. More specifically, this essay is especially helpful to anyone interested in understanding the relationship of religion to public and private life in a fallen world.

Alan R. Crippen II
The Witherspoon Fellowship
Washington, D.C.
Ash Wednesday, 2000

1

INTRODUCTION

On July 29, 1804, Eliphalet Nott stood before his New York congregation and felt the great weight of his task. Like so many ministers across the young nation, the Presbyterian pastor was endeavoring to address a grieving public. Newspapers, civic postings, and rumors had, by then, informed the nation of the tragic death of Alexander Hamilton. The great architect of the *Federalist*, pioneering treasury secretary, renowned lawyer and polemicist, military general, and father of eight was dead at the age of forty-seven. Details of his horrific duel with Vice President Aaron Burr made word of Hamilton's demise all the more calamitous.

"Before such an audience, and on such an occasion," began Nott, "I enter on the duty assigned me with trembling." For his text, the minister selected 2 Samuel 1:19 where David laments the deaths of Saul and Jonathan: "Your glory, O Israel, lies slain on your heights. How the mighty have fallen!"[1] Taking his cue from David's powerful cry, Nott titled his sermon, "How are the Mighty Fallen!" The text fit the moment.

Days before, Hamilton had lain in bed at the home of a friend. A bullet had torn a trail through his abdomen and lodged in his spine, and he was nearing death. Friends and family attended him as doctors lamented the gravity of his wounds. Hamilton's wife, Betsy, was overcome with emotion. Conscious of her hysterics, Hamilton attempted to calm her by urging, "Remember, my Eliza, you are a Christian."[2] The thirty hours between the duel and Hamilton's death were charged with fear and grief for all present. Hamilton, however, is said to have maintained in his conscious hours his usual

---

1. Eliphalet Nott, *A Discourse Delivered in the City of Albany, Occasioned by the Ever to be Lamented Death of Gen. Alexander Hamilton, July 29, 1804* (Albany: Websters and Skinner, 3rd ed., 1806), p. 3.

Alexander Hamilton.

composure and presence of mind. In this state he summoned the energy to await one final visitor, Benjamin Moore, the Episcopal bishop of New York.

Hamilton did not request Moore's presence merely so he would have a saintly hand to hand as he edged toward death. Instead, Hamilton yearned to receive as a final sacrament the service of Holy Communion. With Moore he discussed the truths of his personal faith, acknowledged communion as an affirmation of his "reliance on the mercy of God in Christ," and received the bread and the cup one final time. With his eye on the heavens, "[Hamilton's] last act, more than any other, sheds glory on his character. Everything else death effaces. Religion alone abides with him on his death bed. He dies a Christian."[3]

In death, a Christian, but what of his life? Because Hamilton lived the life of a commanding public figure, he is remembered and studied as such. His life is the story of a statesman, a thinker, a writer, and a soldier. In these and many other areas, he may appear more of a force than a figure. His talents and tireless drive fueled things greater than himself. This public passion and depth tend to eclipse the contours of the private Hamilton, making his story chiefly a political and public one. Still, one cannot help but wonder what forces lay stirring within. Historians of the 1950s were moved to pose the question: Was Alexander Hamilton a Christian statesman?[4] There was and is no easy sound bite to offer as an answer. The vastness of

2. Harold C. Syrett and Jean G. Cooke, ed., *Interview in Weehawken*, (Middletown, Connecticut: Wesleyan University Press, 1960), p. 164.

3. Nott, *A Discourse Delivered*, p. 20.

4. Douglass Adair with Marvin Harvey, "Was Alexander Hamilton a Christian Statesman?" *William & Mary Quarterly*, 3rd Series, 12 (April 1955): 308–329.

the figure precludes any simple brushstrokes of his political views, much less his spiritual life. Like the Reverend John Witherspoon, the great Princeton president, moral philosopher, and leader of leaders whose influence permeated a generation of founders, Hamilton defies classification.

Alexander Hamilton is said by some who study him and by some who knew him to be among the greatest of Americans. Yet he is honored with no marble monument on the order of those celebrating his contemporaries, as his place in history is all too often reduced to a few milestones.

In death and in life Alexander Hamilton was, indeed, mighty and fallen. He soared as a genius across many disciplines, he stumbled as a man in the grip of nature's leanings, and he left behind a journey of redemption. Because "the life-story of the nation is best written and reflected in the lives of its great men," the story of Hamilton needs telling.[5] In recalling his memory our nation might again tremble, not for what was lost in his death, but for what was gained by his life. The redemption of the mighty inevitably yields a tale of instruction and inspiration.

---

5. Arthur Hendrick Vandenberg, *The Greatest American: Alexander Hamilton* (New York: G. P. Putnam's Sons, 1921), p. 10.

2

FROM NOWHERE

Alexander Hamilton's background gave him an awkward identity that was an obstacle to him throughout his life. With so many odds against him, he should never have achieved what he did. He defied status quo assumptions and carved out his own destiny. He was, in short, shocking.

Hamilton's life did not start in America or in Europe. Nor was it built on platforms of nobility, wealth, or strong family ties. He benefited from no momentum to carry him into a life of significance. Instead, he began his journey as an illegitimate child on an obscure island in the British West Indies. His mother was Rachel Faucett, a young woman of French Huguenot lineage whose family lived on the West Indies island of Nevis. While she was still in her teens, her family decided that Rachel would do well to marry John Michael Lavien, a planter and merchant on the nearby Danish island of St. Croix. Marrying well, unfortunately, did not necessarily mean a good marriage; in Rachel's case the endeavor started on weak terms and only grew worse. When she decided that living in the same house with her husband was too much to bear, he determined to have her imprisoned. Technically still married, Rachel soon thereafter fled back to Nevis and began a fifteen-year romance with James Hamilton, the son of a wealthy Scottish landowner. James tried to make his fortune as an upstart merchant while Rachel bore him two sons, first James Jr., then Alexander in 1757.[1] In 1765 the makeshift family moved to St. Croix. In her absence, John Lavien had divorced

Nevis Island in the West Indies circa 1710.

---

1. Historians dispute the exact date of Alexander Hamilton's birth. Some claim a 1755 birthday, but Hamilton himself claimed 1757. Most recent biographers accept the latter.

Map Division, Library of Congress.

St. Croix in the West Indies in 1799.

Rachel in 1759, accusing her of "whoring with everyone."[2] (Under Danish law, she was not allowed to remarry since she was deemed an adulterer.) The saga continued when James dropped out of the picture, leaving Rachel and the boys to fend for themselves. Within a few years, Rachel fell into a severe fever and died.

By any standard in any century, these were ugly beginnings for young Alexander. The men in his early years could never be called role models; his mother had a run of poor judgments and misfortune. Yet the boy did have a loyal admiration for his mother's strong sense of pride, disciplined work ethic, and shrewd business sense; he would later describe her to his own children as having "superior intellect," "elevated and generous sentiments," and "unusual elegance of person and manner."[3] But his own hopeful outlook could not overcome the disgrace of her improprieties. One wonders what island gossip was murmured about the "Lavien woman" and her two fatherless boys. Even uglier for Alexander was the fact that these beginnings would forever define him. In an American culture that afforded honor and respect to pedigree, Hamilton bore the stigma of illegitimacy. Contemporaries like John Adams, who at different times admired and resented Hamilton, would refer to him as "the bastard brat of a Scot's peddler."

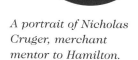

Christiansted National Historic Site.

A portrait of Nicholas Cruger, merchant mentor to Hamilton.

Life on St. Croix carried with it a sense of isolation tempered by heavy commercial activity in its ports. The

---

2. Robert Hendrickson, *The Rise and Fall of Alexander Hamilton* (New York: Van Nostrand Reinhold Co., 1981), p. 8.

3. As quoted in Richard Brookhiser, *Alexander Hamilton, American* (New York: Free Press, 1999), p. 17.

Map of the British West Indies and Mexico, circa 1710

island was larger than Nevis and boasted a population of twenty-four thousand people. Plantation owners and commercial traders typically did well by harvesting and shipping sugar cane that could be processed into sugar or rum. The island resources drew a diverse collection of ambitious European adventurers. Christiansted, the main port, bustled with lively trade. But if the area had a cosmopolitan feel, it was a mediocre one at best. The pragmatism of commercial gain governed life. Slaves made up a large portion of the population and were subject to the interests of the island's two thousand white Europeans.

The setting honed Alexander's sensitivities and whetted his appetite for the rest of the world. He took up work in Christiansted with a merchant named Nicholas Cruger. Originally from New York, Cruger made frequent trading runs as a part of a larger family business. Alexander's duties were to assist him as a clerk in the Christiansted business operations; he wrote letters, compiled trade information, and kept tabs on the cargoes loaded and unloaded from Cruger's ships. It was a humble start, but Hamilton dove into the work with tremendous ambition. He grew in Cruger's confidence and his responsibilities rapidly increased. Meanwhile, the coming and going of ships and the exchanges of business correspondence with overseas contacts enlarged his vision of the rest of the world. St. Croix seemed smaller as the opportunities across the sea grew all the more wondrous.

One of his good friends from Christiansted, Edward Stevens, was sent to New York for schooling at King's College (later Columbia University). Alexander wrote to him on November 11, 1769:

> To confess my weakness, Ned, my ambition is so prevalent that I contemn the grov'ling and condition of a Clerk or the like, to which my Fortune &c. condemns me and would willingly risk my life tho' not my Character to exalt my Station. . . . I'm no Philosopher, you see, and may be justly said to Build Castles in the Air . . . yet Neddy we have seen such Schemes successful when the Projector is Constant I shall conclude saying I wish there was a War.[4]

The longing for things higher than the "groveling condition of a clerk" was combined with Alexander's early grasp of things transcendent. He penned poems and made an effort to publish his writings in the main newspaper of the islands, the *Royal Danish-American Gazette*.

The street in Christiansted, St. Croix, where Hamilton clerked for merchant Nicholas Cruger.

Masthead of the Royal Danish-American Gazette.

4. Harold C. Syrett, ed., *The Papers of Alexander Hamilton,* 25 vols. (New York: Columbia University Press, 1961–77), 1:4.

When a massive hurricane wrought destruction on St. Croix, fifteen-year-old Alexander found his perfect inspiration. His letter appeared in the Gazette as "by a Youth of this Island." He began with a vivid description then caught his breath to offer some somber reflections:

> The roaring of the sea and wind—fiery meteors flying about it in the air—the prodigious glare of a and unruffled temper, we call a natural cause, seemed then like the correction of the almost perpetual lightening—the crash of falling houses. . . . That which in calm Deity. . . . The father and benefactor were forgot, a consciousness of our guilt filled us with despair.[5]

The title page of a theological tract about the 1772 St. Croix hurricane written by Hugh Knox, the Presbyterian minister who served as Hamilton's early spiritual director.

What surfaces as a dramatic conception of the "Deity" in the letter was more than rhetoric. Alexander's voice was giving expression to a larger formation taking place within. One clue to this was his growing friendship with Hugh Knox, a Scottish Presbyterian minister educated at the College of New Jersey (later Princeton University). Knox practiced medicine, wrote theological tracts, and considered his high calling to serve as a "patron who draws genius out of obscurity."[6] After arriving on St. Croix in the spring of 1772 to start his ministry, he was introduced to Alexander and immediately took notice of the boy's talents. Perhaps Cruger and others could not help but showcase the sharp-minded clerk; soon arrangements were made for Knox to tutor Alexander.

If young Hamilton's clerkship for Cruger was an education in world commerce, his interactions with Knox would open a door to even broader and deeper lessons. This would be his first experience with formal education, but there was no question Alexander had made learning a personal discipline. During his early years he had pored through books

---

5. Ibid., 1:35–38.

6. As quoted in Forrest McDonald, *Alexander Hamilton: A Biography* (New York: W. W. Norton & Co., 1979), p. 10.

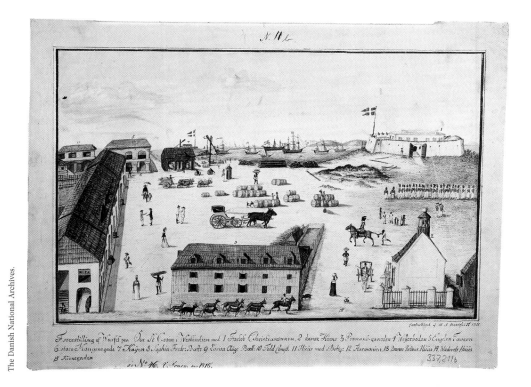

An early colonial settlement on St. Croix Island.

obtained from his mother's thirty-four-volume library. Pope and Plutarch particularly affected him. To this foundation Knox added a healthy dose of seminary education, schooling Alexander in Calvinist doctrine and moral consciousness. He "impressed upon [Hamilton] the dangers of drinking to excess, and taught him to abhor slavery as the wellspring of many other evils."[7]

The student eagerly absorbed his lessons, spiritual and otherwise. More than a century later, Henry Cabot Lodge romantically illustrated the boy's unique talents for learning: "But that which strikes us most at the outset is his extraordinary precocity; his mind and character seemed to partake of the nature of those luxuriant tropical plants which in a few months attain a growth permitted only after years of conflict and care in the harsher climate of the North."[8] Another historian similarly put it: "Born in that tropical region, the brain of this wonderful youth flowered with the

---

7. Ibid., p.10.

8. Henry Cabot Lodge, *Alexander Hamilton* (New York: Greenwood Press, Publishers, 1917), p. 1.

Alexander Hamilton

amazing swiftness of the vegetation around him."[9]

Knox's years in New Jersey had instilled in him the growing political ideas of American Presbyterians. Knox was a "thoroughgoing New Sides man" in the New England camp of those on their way to taking up the charge of revolution.[10] As Hamilton gained from Knox theologically, he may very well have taken in seeds of the Presbyterian's political outlook. But while the pupil's mind opened up to these new sensitivities, his immediate world remained unchanged. This young leader-to-be was stuck on an island in the middle of nowhere.

Writing kept pace with Hamilton's learning. A poem attributed to Hamilton later appeared in the *Gazette*, bearing the title "The Soul ascending into Bliss, In humble imitation of Pope's Dying Christian to his Soul." In the last verse, he exclaimed:

> O Lamb of God! thrice gracious Lord
> Now, now I feel how true thy word;
> Translated to this happy place,
> This blessed vision of thy face;
> My soul shall all thy steps attend
> In songs of triumph without end.[11]

Knox, Cruger, and others close to the boy resolved to open up his world to things beyond the island. Arrangements were made for him to go to the mainland and to college. There he would find a larger landscape for his talents to explore. There, as he had unknowingly foretold in the letter to Ned, he would get his war.

---

9. Edward S. Ellis, *Alexander Hamilton: A Character Sketch* (Chicago: The University Association, 1898), p. 5.

10. McDonald, *Alexander Hamilton*, p. 11.

11. *Hamilton Papers*, 1:38–39.

3

A VISIT WITH JOHN WITHERSPOON

Later in 1772, Hamilton boarded a ship, named *Thunderbolt*, for New York via Boston. If he was at all nervous about the life that awaited him amongst the fiery colonists, no signs suggested it. He was determined and he was ambitious, much like the New World that he entered.

Like St. Croix, New York was a settlement shaped by trade. The population was close to twenty-five thousand—quite large by standards of the time. From its Dutch origins to its use as an English port, New York's identity was always that of a commercial venture. In this world of possibility, Hamilton's own enterprise was to gain a foothold and launch himself toward whatever heights his talents could reach. The obscurity of his origins was still a recent memory and a reminder to clutch the opportunities at hand. Unlike other foreigners, who came with ease to America from superpowers across the sea, "his trajectory was different: he was coming from the fringes to the center."[1]

A 1789 map of New York City drawn by John McComb Jr. Seventeen years after Hamilton's arrival, the city was confined to the lower tip of Manhattan and was bordered on the north by farms.

Patriot, Presbyterian layman, member of the Continental Congress, governor of New Jersey, and delegate to the Constitutional Convention, William Livingston (1723–1790) was an advisor to Hamilton in his teens.

Below: A 1777 letter from Hamilton to Livingston.

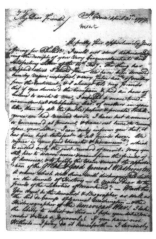

The short-term strategy consisted of a few deliberate steps. Upon arrival in New York, Hamilton was received by friends of Cruger and Knox. They were to shepherd him, enrolling him in grammar school so as to complete his requirements for entering the College of New Jersey, Knox's alma mater.

William Livingston and Elias Boudinot were among Hamilton's chief contacts and became his loyal advisors. Both were devout Presbyterian laymen of considerable influence; both were graduates of the College of New Jersey. It was networking at its best. From the start, the fifteen-year-old's ambitions were not merely personal ambitions, but corporate hopes. He had backing from well-connected people, Whig leaders who schooled Hamilton in the virtues of republican principles. Livingston would soon become Revolutionary governor of New Jersey; Boudinot was an activist for independence and later president of the Continental Congress. Religious virtues similarly ran deep.

The spiritual formation begun under Hugh Knox continued under these new mentors, for, as one historian deduced, "[neither] of these men would have backed a youth who showed signs of religious heterodoxy."[2]

At the Elizabethtown Academy across the harbor from New York, Hamilton sped through a two-year course-load in less than one. Admission at Princeton required, among other things, "the ability to

---

1. Brookhiser, *Alexander Hamilton*, pp. 20–21.
2. Adair and Harvey, "Was Hamilton a Christian Statesman," p. 313.

write Latin prose, translate Vergil, Cicero, and the Greek gospels, and a commensurate knowledge of Latin and Greek grammar."[3] The ambitious student studied in his room until midnight and early in the morning before school began. When he was not cloistered with his books, Hamilton enjoyed the company of the Livingston family and friends in their Elizabethtown mansion, "Liberty Hall." Here he was first introduced to as the budding New York lawyer and 1764 King's College graduate John Jay.

Having mastered the Academy's courses and eager to move on to his next educational feast, Hamilton set out to enroll at Princeton. The college was, at the time, a Presbyterian seminary also serving the purpose of training future republican leaders. Theology still reigned as the queen of the sciences, as the eighty-five students were given a sound biblical framework from which their *knowing* could be translated into Christian *doing*. This was the school that had produced Hugh Knox and this was the education Hamilton desired. Obtaining enrollment was no easy task, even for someone as bright as Hamilton. Qualified as he was, he still had to meet the full approval of the college president, John Witherspoon.

Four years earlier, the Scottish minister had taken up the yoke of leading a school that occupied a "position of paramount importance" in the colonies. He was an impressive leader and a forceful intellectual, and "even his political ideals

Prints and Photographs Division, Library of Congress.

A miniature portrait of Hamilton as a teenager in 1773.

were admirably suited to a country that was hurrying toward its independence."[4] From under his tutelage emerged twelve members of the Continental Congress, five delegates to the Constitutional Convention, one president, one vice president, forty-nine representatives, twenty-eight senators, and three Supreme Court justices. Witherspoon himself would be the only clergyman to sign the Declaration of Independence. His trade at the college was to train young men in theology and philosophy, equipping them

---

3. As quoted in McDonald, *Alexander Hamilton*, p. 12.
4. Sydney E. Ahlstrom, *A Religious History of the American People* (New Haven: Yale University Press, 1972) pp. 274–75.

Kings College (later Columbia University) on its opening day in 1754.

for the work their country would require of them. Whatever field Hamilton was destined for, Witherspoon was the man for him to see.

Neither Hamilton nor Witherspoon ever recalled in detail their feelings about the event. Hercules Mulligan, one of Hamilton's friends at the time, later told the story as he remembered it:

> I went with him to Princeton to the House of Dr. Witherspoon, then the president of the College, with whom I was well acquainted, and I introduced Mr. Hamilton to him and proposed to him to examine the young gentleman which the Doctor did to his entire satisfaction. Mr. Hamilton then stated that he wished to enter either of the classes to which his attainments would entitle him but with the understanding that he should be permitted to advance from Class to Class with as much rapidity as his exertions would enable him to do. Dr. Witherspoon listened with great attention to so unusual a proposi-

tion from so young a person and replied that he had not the sole power to determine but that he would submit the request to the trustees who would decide, which was done & in about a fortnight after a letter was received from the President stating that the request could not be complied with because it was contrary to the usage of the College and expressing his regret because he was convinced that the young gentleman would do honor to any seminary at which he should be educated.[5]

The Reverend Myles Cooper, president of King's College when Hamilton enrolled. An articulate loyalist, the Anglican clergyman argued that the patriots would "open a door for Anarchy, confusion, and every evil work to enter."

As Mulligan noted, Hamilton's request was an unusual one. The young scholar did not hope merely to enroll, but intended to sail through the curriculum at his own swift pace, as he had at Elizabethtown. Mulligan's account suggests that Witherspoon was impressed with Hamilton and even regretful that enrollment was not meant to be. Another concern may have also been afoot. Six years ahead of Hamilton, one of Witherspoon's prized students, a young man from Virginia by the name of James Madison, had essentially done what Hamilton was asking to do. Richard Brookhiser writes, "Brilliant and industrious, he had gone through Princeton in two years, after which he suffered a nervous collapse. Perhaps memories of the episode discouraged Dr. Witherspoon from letting Hamilton study at his own pace." Whatever the case, Witherspoon's college was not in Hamilton's cards. Yet fortune would later return him to Princeton in January 1777, when Hamilton the soldier fired artillery at the college's Nassau Hall to liberate it from the British.[6]

Denied by Princeton but undeterred in his ambitions, Hamilton took his

5. Nathan Schachner, "Alexander Hamilton Viewed by His Friends: The Narratives of Robert Troup and Hercules Mulligan," *William and Mary Quarterly*, 3rd Series, 4 (1947): 209.

6. Brookhiser, *Alexander Hamilton*, p. 52. Ralph Edward Bailey tells the story: "At the Battle of Princeton, he had, according to Trevelyan, 'with the irreverence of a student fresh from a rival place of education, planted his guns on the sacred grass of the academical campus, and fired a six pound shot, which is said to have passed through the head of King George the Second's portrait in the chapel." *An American Colossus: The Singular Career of Alexander Hamilton* (Boston: Lothrop, Lee & Shepard, 1933), p. 58.

offer to King's College in New York. While Princeton was a stronghold of Presbyterianism, King's leaned heavily toward Anglicanism. The gatekeeper this time was President Myles Cooper, a loyal Anglican, who agreed to Hamilton's terms. Once again Hamilton hit the ground running: "He was studious, and made rapid progress in the languages, and every other branch of learning, to which he applied himself."[7] He met requirements in formal classes with the college's four faculty members, including Cooper, and also through private tutoring. Originally interested in the field of medicine, the young scholar frequented lectures on anatomy given by Samuel Clossey. King's library, which housed works of legal and political philosophy (including volumes of Locke, Montesquieu, and Hume), was also a compelling draw. Whatever the subject matter, his studious discipline enabled him to devour the King's curriculum in "huge gulps," taking less than two-and-a-half years to complete the sum of his course requirements.[8]

Outside of class, Hamilton kept up with the Boudinot family and from time to time joined them in their family devotions, offering prayers and penning verses of poetry laced with spiritual sympathies. On his own, he was similarly stirred to routines of private prayer and Anglican worship. Robert Troup, his roommate and lifelong friend, provided these recollections years after Hamilton's death:

> Whilst at College, the General was attentive to public worship; and in the habit of praying upon his knees both night and morning. I lived in the same Room with him for sometime; and I have often been powerfully affected, by the fervor and eloquence of his prayers. The General had read most of the polemical writers on Religious subjects; and he was a zealous believer in the fundamental doctrines of Christianity; and I confess, that the arguments with which he was accustomed to justify his belief, have tended, to no small degree, to confirm my own faith in revealed Religion.[9]

Hugh Knox might have raised an eyebrow at the Anglican cast, but Hamilton's candid Christian devotion would no doubt have encouraged him.

Hamilton was not one to be lukewarm in any interest. With several colleagues, including Ned Stevens, Hamilton embarked on a club "for our improvement in composition—in debating—and in public speaking." One

---

7. Schachner, "Hamilton Viewed by His Friends," p. 212.
8. McDonald, *Alexander Hamilton*, p. 12.
9. Schachner, "Hamilton Viewed by His Friends," p. 213.

club member recalled that Hamilton "made extraordinary displays of richness of genius, and energy of mind."[10] When he was not amazing his companions, he had a habit of "puzzling pedestrians by talking to himself as he walked for hours each day under the great trees of Bateau (Dey) Street."[11] He would investigate intellectual problems, rehearse lessons, and compose papers aloud, all while strolling along unconcerned by the curious stares and whispers of passersby. The habit stayed with him into his adult years.

But Hamilton was not so lost in thought that he was oblivious to the ideas and events whirling about him. Just two months after he entered King's, the Boston Tea Party raised colonial fervor against British control. Britain's Coercive Acts came like a sharp blow soon thereafter, and before the end of the year, the First Continental Congress was convened to strategize an embargo on trade. A revolution was brewing. Britain continued to trespass on the rights of the colonists, so it seemed, and the public mind was spurred beyond restraint. Questions of loyalty were raised. Understanding his times, Hamilton had some decisions to make.

One of the trickier currents to navigate was the age-old whirlpool of politics and faith. The fact that political and church loyalties were typically muddled together helped start a lifetime of ecclesiastical confusion for Hamilton. The spiritual formation that had taken place under Hugh Knox in St. Croix and under Boudinot and Livingston at Elizabethtown was of the Presbyterian sort; it was Christian nourishment with a helping of revolutionary passion on the side. Had Hamilton been taken into the Princeton fold, this correlation would certainly have continued and perhaps solidified in his mind. But at King's, he was in the company of Anglicans, and Anglicanism was firmly on the side of the crown. Anglicanism clearly left its imprint on Hamilton's developing faith. But, unlike Dr. Cooper of the College, his roots were not so deep in the political allegiances of the Church of England, as the revolutionary fervor of Presbyterian Whigs compelled him.

Perhaps on one of his regular strolling conversations with himself, Hamilton may have sorted through the electrified passions of the historical moment. One can imagine the young immigrant from the islands recalling the days when he first conceived of a world outside St. Croix, now surveying the New York world around him and reveling in his new arena. "The ardour

---

10. Ibid., pp. 212–13.

11. As quoted in Claude G. Bowers, *Jefferson and Hamilton: The Struggle for Democracy in America* (Boston and New York: Houghton Mifflin, 1925), p. 25.

of his feelings clothed every object of his attention with a powerful interest," wrote John C. Hamilton of his father, "and the wise instruction of his youth had taught him that the flame of devotion does not burn less purely for being kindled on the same altar with the fires of a virtuous emulation."[12] He had a spirit of devotion and a storehouse of ambition, and to these he added impassioned reason—a quality that would mark his life. All three reckoned with the fact that the war he had longed for as a clerk in Christiansted was taking shape on the horizon. Lodge, with a touch of appropriate drama, summarized Hamilton's moment:

> His clear, vigorous mind and his profound belief in reasoning and argument, which so prevailed with him always, showed him plainly that the colonies were right. . . . He was young, unknown, an adventurer in a strange land, and burning with lofty ambition. The world was before him, and his fortune . . . was to be made.[13]

When the great hurricane had decimated his homeland, the young Alexander had taken up his pen and made a name for himself. With a storm of rebellion blowing into the colonies, the seventeen-year-old Hamilton would once again seize his day and cement his fortune. His primary means of engagement would be—then and throughout the whole of his public life—the power of words.

---

12. John C. Hamilton, *The Life of Alexander Hamilton* (New York: Halsted & Voorhies, 1834), p. 10.

13. Lodge, *Alexander Hamilton*, pp. 6–7.

The South Prospect of the City of New York in America

4

AT GEORGE WASHINGTON'S SIDE

In the winter of 1774, Hamilton produced two stirring essays defending the actions of the First Continental Congress and deconstructing the loyalist cause: "A Full Vindication of the Measures of Congress" and "The Farmer Refuted." He signed these pamphlets under the auspices of "A Friend of America." In the essays, he grappled with prevailing concerns, arguing in one passage against Parliament's unbridled right to tax the colonies:

> No reason can be advanced why one man should exercise any power or pre-eminence over his fellow-creatures more than another, unless they have voluntarily vested him with it. Since, then, Americans have not, by any act of theirs, empowered the British Parliament to make laws for them, it follows they can have no just authority to do it.[1]

Not only was he savvy on the issues at hand, but he also had the ability to inspire. Another passage shows a depth of philosophy, even poetry:

> The sacred rights of mankind are not to be rummaged for among old parchments or musty records. They are written, as with a sunbeam, in the whole volume of human nature, by the hand of divinity himself.[2]

Running between fifty and sixty thousand words altogether, the two pamphlets thundered impressively across New England. Many patriots

---

1. As quoted in Anson D. Morse, "Alexander Hamilton," *Political Science Quarterly* 5 (March 1890): 2–3.
2. Ibid.

Colonel Hamilton at the siege of Yorktown, Virginia, in 1781.

thought John Jay had to be their author because they were of such great quality. But soon enough Hamilton withdrew his veil; the public—not to mention prominent revolutionary figures—was astonished by his youth. At seventeen years of age, he was already thinking like a statesman. He mastered facts and argued from principles with such force that, as one early historian announced, "these papers deserve high rank in the political literature of the Revolution."[3]

Words continued to carry him into the revolutionary arena; "his perspicacity, penetration, powers of condensation, and clarity of expression were those of a premier editorial writer." In addition to writing, he was speaking at patriotic meetings, "swaying crowds with argument despite his delicate, boyish appearance."[4] Hugh Knox would have been proud. The island prodigy imbued the revolutionary cause with both passion and prudence, advocating moderation in dealing with Tories, opposing mob rule, and affirming civil rights.[5] Activism ran through his veins, but, like Jay, he consistently wedded it to reason. When bands of Patriot radicals took extreme measures against New York Loyalists, Hamilton voiced his alarm to Jay:

> When the minds of these [men] are loosened from their attachment to ancient establishments and courses, they seem to grow giddy and are apt more or less to run into anarchy. . . In such tempestuous times, it requires the greatest skill in the political pilots to keep men steady and within the proper bounds.[6]

A thinker, a writer, and even an ideological leader, the college boy was off to a quick start. But would he prove himself on the "tooth and nail" testing ground of the day—the battlefield? He hoped so. When King's College, threatened on account of its Loyalist affiliation, closed for the revolution, Hamilton was already as adept with his musket and military drills as he was deft with logic and words. Military readiness was vital to New Yorkers who had toppled the royal government in February 1776, fully

---

3. Ibid, p. 3.

4. Bowers, *Jefferson and Hamilton*, p. 25.

5. McDonald, *Alexander Hamilton*, p. 13. When a revolutionary mob assailed the house of King's College President Myles Cooper, a Loyalist, Hamilton set aside his political affinities and "harangued the mob long enough for Cooper to exit by a back gate, soon to take refuge on a British warship in the Hudson, sail for England, and publicly acknowledge young Hamilton's role in saving his hide." Richard B. Morris, *Witnesses at the Creation: Hamilton, Madison, Jay, and the Constitution* (New York: Holt, Rinehart and Winston, 1985), p. 33.

6. As quoted in Mary-Jo Kline, ed., *Alexander Hamilton: A Biography in His Own Words* (New York: Newsweek, 1973), pp. 45–46.

Hamilton's commission as a lieutenant colonel in the United States Army with his rank dated March 1, 1777.

The page pictured above is taken from the army pay book that became Hamilton's personal note pad and journal.

expecting a British invasion of their province in the coming spring.

Hamilton's military years, lasting from one month after his nineteenth birthday until two months before his twenty-fifth, marked his "coming of age." He was like his nation in this regard. The pace was swift and the stakes were great. By March 1776 he was captain of an artillery company and took to the field as a boy leading men. A battle observer reported seeing Hamilton in action, "a youth, a mere stripling, small, slender, almost delicate in frame," marching forward with his "cocked hat pulled down over his eyes, apparently lost in thought, with his hand resting on a cannon, and every now and then patting it, as if it were a favorite horse or a pet plaything." His disciplined resolve, along with his intellectual stamina, French fluency, self-assurance, and "socially impeccable sponsorship among the Patriots" proved powerful assets; his reputation grew.[7] Within the year General George Washington recruited him to his personal staff as an aide-de-camp with the rank of lieutenant colonel. As Hamilton matured, he "shot up like a skyrocket," winning fame as a soldier, respect as a leader, and renown as a crack administrator mastermind in the great general's organization.[8]

Troop movements, continental supply lines, pay allocations, official correspondence, and diplomatic politics likely afforded little time for pensive strolls and dabbling in things transcendent. Hamilton's mind remained hungry and his spirit active, nevertheless. An army pay-book became his personal note pad and journal, leaving history a few fragments of the

7. Morris, *Witnesses at the Creation*, p. 34.
8. Adair and Harvey, "Was Hamilton a Christian Statesman?" p. 314.

ideas and observations swirling about in his head. In a time that magnified the need for leadership, to find him thinking deeply about classical teachings on the subject is not surprising; on one page of the notes he penned a quote from Demosthenes:

> As a general marches at the head of his troops, so ought wise politicians, if I dare use the expression, to march at the head of affairs; insomuch that they ought not to wait the event, to know what measures to take; but the measures which they have taken ought to produce the event.[9]

Hamilton tried to apply this idea as a soldier. After securing his post as an artillery captain, for example, the young leader had managed to recruit his own company of sixty-eight officers and men, footing the bill for all the clothing and equipment. Demosthenes' axiom was to permeate his statesmanship in the years to come; observers would take notice of his uncanny foresight. One admirer of his economic and political wisdom would remark that Hamilton "anticipated America," still another that he "anticipated Europe."[10]

Also on the pay book's pages was a telling observation he made of Plutarch's essay, "Life of Numa Pompilius," in his *Lives of the Noble Gracious and Roman:*

> He (Numa) was a wise prince and went a great way in civilizing the Romans. The chief engine he employed for this purpose was religion, which could alone have

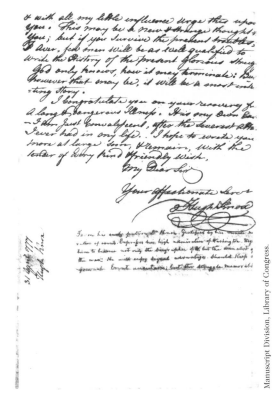

A letter, dated April 31, 1777, from the Reverend Hugh Knox, encouraging Hamilton to write a history of "the present glorious struggle" (the Revolutionary War) adding, "God only knows how it may terminate."

---

9. Richard B. Morris, ed., *Alexander Hamilton and the Founding of the Nation* (New York: The Dial Press, 1957), p. xi.

10. Ibid., pp. xi–xii.

sufficient empire over the minds of a barbarous and warlike people to engage them to cultivate the arts of peace.[11]

Religion could be a positive vehicle for civilization—it could turn the tide of even a "barbarous" people. Political problems with church loyalties aside, this made sense to Hamilton. The Roman prince offered one illustration of Demosthenes' charge, and Hamilton would not forget the lesson.

For now, however, the energy and opportunities of war took first priority in Hamilton's mind. For this reason, his faith during these years is not easy to catalog. Robert Troup remembered that Hamilton's prayer habits, first observed while at King's, continued as he entered the army:

A romanticized engraving of General Washington carrying the colors at the Battle of Princeton, January 3, 1777.

When [Hamilton] commanded a company of Artillery in the summer of 1776, I paid him a visit; and at night, and in the morning, he went to prayer in his usual mode. Soon after this visit we were parted by our respective duties in the Army, and we did not meet again before 1779.[12]

Without further reports from Troup, any efforts to draw conclusions about Hamilton's spiritual life are guesswork at best. Church-going routines are no clear indicator either, since these were the days when a man had to "purchase" his spot on the pew. The fairest assumption is that the soldier's faith was neither dormant nor buoyant. He was by no means indifferent to the Christian pulse of his blood, even though he was not one who wore his faith on his sleeve.

History remembers him most during this time as being driven by ambition. Ambition is never easy to evaluate. For Hamilton, one great object of ambition was winning the respect that comes with bravery. He also cared about winning the war, as liberty had to be

---

11. Adair and Harvey, "Was Hamilton a Christian Statesman," p. 317.

12. Schachner, "Hamilton Viewed by His Friends," p. 213.

purchased with bravery. Forrest McDonald explains that "in his prewar polemics [Hamilton] had written, 'there is a certain enthusiasm in liberty, that makes human nature rise above itself, in acts of bravery and heroism' and predicted that such 'animation' would be enough to overcome Britain's advantage of having a professional army."[13]   While an active soldier, the young patriot displayed this confidence and performed heroic acts that did indeed win him fame. Well into his first combat experience, for example, he risked the shower of enemy fire simply to retrieve a musket that had been left behind. As an officer, he once went so far as to put his men through the manual of arms while knowingly within open range of the enemy. This blend of bravery and hubris was the "cast of mind" for many officers of the time who prized honor and pushed the envelope to obtain it. Ambition also kept Hamilton in a perennial hurry, always surging forward to the next thing. His faith, then, may have had a struggle to keep up during this time.

Four years as an aide-de-camp to Washington were a strenuous apprenticeship and frequently kept Hamilton on the go. He was at the center of military decision-making and his administrative know-how increased dramatically. "Much as he yearned to prove his worth on the battlefield, he was forced to recognize that he could contribute far more as an administrator—for he was a man who could run things, and that talent was in great demand and short supply."[14] By managing various administrative affairs, penning much of the general's correspondence, and carrying out numerous special assignments, Hamilton helped provide many of the services comparable to those of a chief of staff. Ever watchful of the enemy's movements, he made a habit of seeing that those who needed information got it. In September 1777, he rushed off a letter to Patrick Henry, the president of Congress, urging him to evacuate the legislature from Philadelphia for fear that Sir William Howe's forces were bearing down on the capital. His commitment to work at headquarters, coupled with his attentiveness to all goings-on in the field, made him indispensable. One contemporary declared, "The pen of our army was held by Hamilton."[15]

Moreover, the military household of Washington made for a humbling and sharpening environment. Alongside the general, Hamilton knew he was in the presence of a man greater than himself. Says Brookhiser, "Hamilton's understanding was quicker than Washington's, and his analytical powers

---

13. McDonald, *Alexander Hamilton*, p. 14.

14. Ibid., p. 15.

15. As quoted in Bowers, *Jefferson and Hamilton*, p. 28.

were greater. But in every other mental or moral quality, Washington was his equal or superior."[16] Washington's greatness was of the most noble sort—a greatness of character. He lived and breathed statesmanship, and set a high bar for Hamilton. The two shared a mutual respect and appreciation. More than twenty years Hamilton's elder, Washington had weathered battlefields before Hamilton even dreamed of war. In Hamilton, Washington appreciated an ambitious flair that may have reminded him of his own early years. And while others chafed under the immense drive of the "Little Lion" (or "the boy," as he was also called), Washington considered Hamilton's ambition to be "of that laudable kind, which prompts a man to excel in whatever he takes in hand."[17]

Hamilton's laudable ambitions also awarded him the hand of a fine lady. When a lull in the New Jersey military action during the winter of 1779-80 freed up the bachelor's social calendar, he undertook the courtship of Elizabeth Schuyler, the daughter of a powerful New York congressman. Writing to his future sister-in-law, Hamilton said of his "Betsey":

> I have already confessed the influence your sister has gained over me. . . . She is most unmercifully handsome . . . and there are several of my friends, philosophers who rallied at love as a weakness, men of the world who laughed at it as a phantasie [sic], whom she has presumptuously and daringly compelled to acknowledge its power and surrender at discretion.[18]

The courtship continued, with Hamilton's visits interspersed between the demands of military duties; the two celebrated an Albany wedding in December 1780. He was, by his own account, a "fanatic in love."[19] Marital bliss, however, was tempered by public duty; the year ahead looked to be a pivotal one of possible military reforms and republic making.

Though continued service on the general's staff enabled Hamilton to unloose his genius for administrative matters, he missed the battlefield. He was disenchanted with the politics of war, numb to his earlier visions of a bold and "animated" struggle, and wanted to be back where he could smell the powder and feel the boom of artillery. Yet Washington was not eager to let him leave the New York headquarters. After four full years of laboring

---

16. Brookhiser, *Alexander Hamilton*, p. 31.

17. Morris, *Witnesses at the Creation*, p. 37.

18. Kline, *Alexander Hamilton*, p. 78.

19. Kline, *Alexander Hamilton*, p. 93.

A reception held by George and Martha Washington upon the marriage of Alexander Hamilton to Elizabeth Schuyler, daughter of the New York grandees General and Mrs. Philip Schuyler.

with him, the general relied on his protégé. Hamilton, however, had begun to feel like the clerk in Cruger's shipping house. He bitterly wrote his father-in-law, Major General Philip Schuyler, of his relationship with Washington: "The truth is our own dispositions are the opposites of each other & the pride of my temper would not suffer me to profess what I did not feel."[20] In April 1781 he resigned as aide-de-camp. The two men would remain respectful friends until Washington's death, but for now they parted.

When October arrived, Hamilton once again led on the field, this time in Yorktown, Virginia. The British manned two strategic posts—known as "redoubts"—near the York River, and the American and French forces needed to bully their way in to take them. Lafayette oversaw plans for the assault on one of the forts and gave Hamilton, his friend, charge of leading four hundred men to get the job done. It was to be a nighttime attack and the odds were not in the revolutionaries' favor. Hamilton took his men through

---

20. Ibid., p.96.

Hamilton's wife, Elizabeth Schuyler Hamilton, at thirty years of age.

Hamilton, Alexander, 1755/57–1804, Statesman, John Trumbull, 1756–1843. Oil on Canvas, 76.2 x 61 cm. (30 x 24 in.), 1806. NPG.79.216. National Portrait Gallery; Smithsonian Institution; Gift of Henry Cabot Lodge.

Alexander Hamilton.

the maze of ditches, bushes, and fallen trees set out as obstacles to such an attack and seized the post, suffering only light casualties. The following day he wrote in his report to Lafayette that "the rapidity and immediate success of the assault are the best comment on the behaviour of the troops. . . . There was not an officer nor soldier whose behaviour, if it could be particularized, would not have a claim to the warmest approbation."[21] He boasted only of his troops' performance, knowing his own honor was evident from the night's achievement and needed no mention.

Five days later, on October 19, Cornwallis surrendered his British armies. Peace treaties were still some way off, but the war was over for Hamilton. He had finished on a sweet note of glory.

---

21. Ibid., pp. 100–101.

5

A Principled Colossus

Yorktown's triumphs may have been a finale for Hamilton's military years, but the arc of his career was still climbing. In a January 1782 report, Congress honored him for his "superior abilities and knowledge of his profession," and recognized that keeping him on board as an asset to the victorious nation's military leadership would be wise.[1] Yet Hamilton had had his war, he was firmly in the arena of American leadership. Where he had once excelled as a soldier and administrator he would now prove his greater worth as a statesman, though military service would resurface years later in 1798 when he was commissioned inspector general of the army.

By 1787, Hamilton's public life had become remarkable for its many acts of public service. He served as a New York delegate to the Continental Congress in 1782, established and operated a law office on an emerging thoroughfare named Wall Street, helped to create the New York Society for Promoting the Manumission of Slaves, founded the Bank of New York, and earned a seat in the New York State Assembly. As an attorney he was "literally a peacemaker" with respected abilities for "sifting right from wrong;" he made it an "invariable rule not to engage in any case unless he thought it had right on its side."[2] His fees were fair, perhaps erring on the side of taking too little at times. He even provided services for his old college parish, Trinity Church.

---

1. Kline, *Alexander Hamilton*, p. 113.

2. The anti-slavery society was a reform movement undertaken with John Jay and several other New Yorkers that successfully pushed to make slavery illegal in New York. Hamilton himself never owned slaves; during the war he proposed with friend John Laurens to raise a regiment of freed slaves, explaining to Jay: "The contempt we have been taught to entertain for the blacks, makes us fancy many things that are founded neither in reason nor experience," Brookhiser, *Alexander Hamilton*, p. 176. See also Schachner, "Hamilton Viewed by His Friends," p. 221.

Trinity Episcopal Church at the head of Wall Street in lower Manhattan. Hamilton was buried in its churchyard on July 14, 1804.

The Pennsylvania State House (later Independence Hall) circa 1778 on Chestnut Street in Philadelphia. This building housed Pennsylvania's colonial government, the Second Continental Congress, the Confederation Congress, Pennsylvania's state government, the U.S. Constitutional Convention of 1787, the organizing General Convention of the Protestant Episcopal Church in 1789, and (in an expanded complex) the government of the United States from 1790 to 1800.

The financial and political affairs of New York kept the rising leader engrossed in issues of governance. Here he again displayed his prowess for organization; more significantly, he was forever making the case for a strong federal government. On the latter point, he believed that the Articles of Confederation were a rope of sand that withheld from the government the very powers it needed to maintain the Union. "Government implies trust," he reminded some of his colleagues, "and every government must be trusted so far as is necessary to enable it to attain the ends for which it is instituted."[3] For the thirteen colonies that had just fought to rid themselves of a king and parliament, the idea of affording a central government more power and trust was not altogether popular. Hamilton had fought for independence because he opposed British policy and favored the colonial cause, but he maintained an undisguised affinity for the ideology embedded in the British Constitution. There was even exaggerated murmuring among critics that this transplant from a West Indies trading station was a closet monarchist. His chance to defend himself and advance his case for governance soon arrived. In May 1787, he took his seat at the Constitutional Convention in Philadelphia.

Philadelphia's famous gathering, and the course it would set for the rest of Hamilton's public life, made his thinking clear: he thought in terms of first things. He was a principled thinker, always positioning himself on absolute points and

---

3. Kline, *Alexander Hamilton*, p. 154.

Alexander Hamilton

building from there. He was never one to wonder among lofty complexities or muse about inevitable progress. His style was to unearth the deepest core truths as he understood them, set them up as formidable pillars, and force the discussion to happen at their base. "He was well grounded in first principles," recalled Troup, "and these the Herculean powers of his genius, enabled him to apply with wonderful facility, to every question he argued."[4] No issue had a superficial answer; no problem existed that could be remedied by political whims. This outlook meant that he cared about bringing the deeper things to the surface of public matters. His hope was always that American government would have a principled character—that virtue would be a matter of habit. A few years prior to the convention he had written:

> Early habits . . . give a lasting bias to the temper and character. Our governments, hitherto, have no habits. How important to the happiness, not of America alone, but of mankind, that they should acquire good ones!

> If we set out with justice, moderation, liberality and a scrupulous regard for the constitution, the government will acquire a spirit and

The 1787 Constitution Convention in the assembly room of the Pennsylvania State House (later Independence Hall) in Philadelphia.

---

4. Schachner, "Hamilton Viewed by His Friends," p. 215.

tone productive of permanent blessings to the community. If, on the contrary, the public councils are guided by humor, passion and prejudice . . . the future spirit of government will be feeble, distracted, and arbitrary.[5]

During the 1787 convention, this emphasis on first things guided Hamilton's thinking on plans for a national government that would cultivate the public good. In the first part of a five-hour speech before the delegates, he hammered out the "great and essential principles necessary for the support of government." He established his framework by asserting that the "great question" for the convention was: "What provision shall we make for the happiness of our country?"[6] According to James Madison's convention notes,

James Madison, father of the Constitution and a co-author of the Federalist Papers *with John Jay and Alexander Hamilton. Later during President Washington's administration, Madison proved to be a formidable political opponent of his Federalist collaborators.*

[Hamilton] agreed moreover . . . that we owed it to our Country, to do on this emergency whatever we should deem essential to its happiness. The states sent us here to provide for the exigencies of the Union. To rely on & propose any plan not adequate to these exigencies. . . would be to sacrifice the means to the end.[7]

The principles necessary for a healthy government were common, even self-explanatory: an active interest in supporting government (as it provides for happiness), an appreciation for the right use of power, an attachment to people, the force of law for positive coercion, and well-directed influence. The trouble, Hamilton argued, was that where states were the primary power base, the principles were debased, becoming misdirected and corrupted passions. State authority drew out man's baser leanings. Only under a strong

---

5. Morse, "Alexander Hamilton," p. 7. Morse comments: "This solicitude for the future and for the world; for the permanent effects of a particular policy upon the character of the people and the government . . . is a strongly marked trait of Hamilton and proves the high quality of his statesmanship."

6. Cecilia M. Kenyon, "Alexander Hamilton: Rousseau of the Right," *Political Science Quarterly* 73 (1958): 162.

7. As quoted in Kline, *Alexander Hamilton*, p. 169.

Alexander Hamilton

federal system interested in union and nationhood could the necessary principles be drawn from among the body of citizens, and happiness achieved. As one historian explains: "In order to make [the principles] support the nation rather than the separate states, Hamilton advocated an almost complete transfer of sovereignty from the latter governments to the former."[8] The minutia of his political science is for another extended discussion—more telling, and more lasting, are the principles underlying his thought.

When viewed beyond the convention in perspective of his whole public life, Hamilton's ideas and objectives were permeated by matters of moral transcendence. He was not making his living in moral philosophy or systematic theology (though he might have), but was a busy man engaged in efforts he felt were imperative to building the nation. His political and social outlook contained three major components.

First, he was committed to the ideal that government must serve to advance the public good. Public happiness was "morally and politically prior to private, individual ends."[9] The focus of government was to be the national interest. Basic and benign as it may sound, this principle was not the prevailing one in political thought of the time. Enlightenment emphasis on natural rights gripped leaders such as Thomas Jefferson and Tom Paine, inclining them more to principles of individual rather than corporate good. Hamilton's view was more classical, stemming in part from "natural law" notions of harmony and consensus for the republic. By no means did he destain individual freedoms and rights, but he roundly opposed the egoism of individualism.

Second, he believed in the depravity of man. Not optimistic about human nature, he cited the passions of men as the driving characteristic of fallen humanity. "His writings are filled with references to what has been called the 'dark side of humanity,'" observes one scholar. "None of his contemporaries excelled him in constant emphasis on self-interest as man's dominant political motive, or in warnings against the evil passions of man's nature."[10] The Anglican Book of Common Prayer may have impressed upon him the doctrine of original sin years before; the world he observed evidently bore witness to the truth of the liturgy. At the convention he

---

8. Hamilton explained: "All the passions then we see, of avarice, ambition, interest, which govern most individuals, and all public bodies, fall into the current of the States, and do not flow in the stream of the General Govt," Kenyon, "Alexander Hamilton," p. 162.

9. Ibid., p. 161.

10. Ibid.

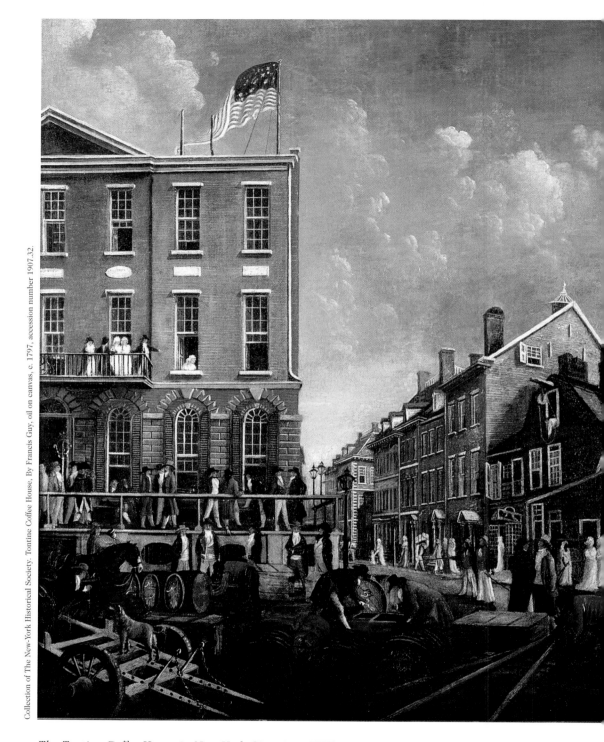

The Tontine Coffee House in New York City circa 1797.

reportedly urged his fellow delegates:

> Take mankind in general, they are vicious . . . and what are they governed by? Their passions. . . . Our prevailing passions are ambition and interest; and it will ever be the duty of a wise government to avail itself of the passions, in order to make them subservient to the public good; for those ever induce us to action.[11]

Third, his sensitivity to the passions that are born out of depravity made him skeptical of democracy's excesses. "Why has government been instituted at all?" he wrote in the *Federalist Papers*. "Because the passions of men will not conform to the dictates of reason and justice, without constraint."[12] Democracy, he lamented, too easily failed to offer the constraint, opening up government to the full throttle of passions and factions. Hence the irony: his paramount objective was the public good, but he believed it was not best pursued by the unbalanced whims of the public mind.

Federal Hall on Wall Street in New York City, the seat of the U.S. government in 1789. President-elect George Washington took his oath of office on its balcony. Trinity Episcopal Church can be viewed in the background.

T. S. Eliot, more recently, observed: "When a term has become so universally sanctified as 'democracy' now is, I begin to wonder whether it means anything, in meaning too many things. . . . If anybody ever attacked democracy, I might discover what the word meant."[13] Hamilton would have sympathized; it concerned him that in a democracy "the voice of the people has been said to be the voice of God; and however generally this maxim has been quoted and believed, it is not true in fact. The people are turbulent and chang-

---

11. Ibid., p. 168.

12. As quoted in Ellis Sandoz, *A Government of Laws: Political Theory, Religion, and the American Founding* (Baton Rouge: Louisiana State University Press, 1990), p. 178.

13. T. S. Eliot, *Christianity and Culture* (New York: Harcourt Brace, 1948), p. 11.

ing; they seldom judge or determine right." Thus, "can a democratic Assembly, who annually revolve around the mass of the people, be supposed steadily to pursue the public good?"[14] His answer was no. This concern was a compelling argument for his belief that the American political system must be as federal and republican as possible.

With these principles, Hamilton campaigned for his grand and detailed vision of the United States. He was as likely to waver on an issue as he was to return to St. Croix. His skin was thick, his confidence robust, and his force jarring. With Madison and Jay he spearheaded the fight for ratification of the Constitution, a document that he believed to be flawed with compromises, but a vast improvement on the flimsy Articles and urgently needed in securing order and direction for the nation. Some scholars believe that Hamilton authored as many as fifty-one of the eighty-five *Federalist Papers.* He also battled the New York Convention in 1788 for ratification of the Constitution. "Without his foresight, energy, and organizational skill," notes one observer, "there would have been no *Federalist* to stiffen the friends of the constitution and to instruct the minds of posterity."[15] If Madison was the father of the Constitution, Hamilton was its supreme lobbyist. He, more than anyone, worked to guarantee its place in American history.

Having won that battle, Hamilton barely had time to catch his breath before President Washington tapped him to be secretary of the treasury, at the age

In order to shore-up an infant nation's capitalist economy, Treasury Secretary Hamilton proposed the establishment of the First Bank of the United States located on Third Street in Philadelphia.

Thomas Jefferson was Alexander Hamilton's political arch nemesis.

---

14. Kenyon, "Alexander Hamilton," p. 163.

15. Clinton Rossiter, ed., *The Federalist Papers* (New York: The New American Library of World Literature, 1961), p. ix; Rossiter poignantly summarizes the thrust of the *Federalist* message: "And the message of *The Federalist* reads: no happiness without liberty, no liberty without self-government, no self-government without constitutionalism, no constitutionalism without morality—and none of these great goods without stability and order," p. xvi.

of thirty-two years. The acute business sense that had begun its formation in his Chistiansted days, coupled with his genius for organization, aided him greatly in his new post. To these abilities he added a keen sense of the politics of national economy, thinking "in terms of world politics at a time when America was creating a new spirit and system of her own."[16] America's finances were in a postwar shambles, but Hamilton foresaw opportunities on the global scale. He tackled the enterprise of establishing America's credit, "propos[ing] to turn the United States into a cash economy. He would lift it into capitalism (a word that did not yet exist) by creating capital."[17] Additional goals and mileposts included his plans for a national bank and his skillful "Report on Manufactures." "In a word," summarized one admirer, "he was the torch of progress." As Lodge explained in 1882, "He armed the government with credit and with a productive revenue. . . . He won for it the hearty good-will of the business world. . . . [It was] the work of a master-mind looking far into the future."[18]

Meanwhile, Hamilton had landed himself at the head of a political movement, the Federalist Party, which took its name and its principles from the collection of essays defending the Constitution. Unionists, constitutionalists, and economists favoring Hamilton's fiscal policies rallied behind firm federal government and the leadership of their favorite American champion, President Washington. Hamilton, whose cabinet role became that of an unofficial prime minister, designed and managed party strategies. As Vandenberg framed the situation, "If Washington was their President, Hamilton was their Generalissimo."[19]

The Federalists defined themselves by their enemies—namely, Thomas Jefferson and his allies. Jefferson was Washington's secretary of state and fourteen years Hamilton's senior. The two exchanged blows in cabinet meetings, in the press, and at the many political crossroads that marked their careers. Though they did not know each other before their first autumn on the cabinet, "Over the next dozen years, [Hamilton] would come to know [Jefferson], to despise him, and to back him for president"—the last event occurring when the only alternative to a Jefferson presidency was Aaron Burr. As a rival, Jefferson was well qualified to comment on Hamilton's forcefulness. He wrote to Madison in the spring of 1795: "Hamilton is really

16. Bowers, *Jefferson and Hamilton*, pp. 36–37.

17. Brookhiser, *Alexander Hamilton*, pp. 85–86.

18. Vandenberg, *The Greatest American*, pp. 87–88.

19. Ibid., p. 89.

20. Brookhiser, *Alexander Hamilton*, pp. 77, 124.

a colossus to the anti-republican [Federalist] party. Without numbers, he is an host within himself."[20]

The colossus was in the public square because his convictions and his tenacity took him there. To be fair, a healthy dose of partisanship and politicking was at work; Hamilton's hands were in it just like everyone else's. But his principles drove him. However much he fought semantics in the press, the great volume of articles and essays he produced

A period engraving of Hamilton with his temptress, Maria Reynolds.

over time arose from his passion for educating public opinion. He was not greatly enthusiastic about the quality of the public mind on its own; he sought to transform it through rhetorical leadership. As Anson Morse put it:

> Any just estimate of Hamilton's work must take into the account what he did for the education of the public. . . . Friends and foes testified that in the qualities which enable a writer to convince, Hamilton was with-out a rival. . . . He wrote, often at considerable length, on every important public question which arose during the Federalist period. . . . Indeed, considering both range and quality, it is scarcely venturesome to say that Hamilton's works exceed in value those of any other American statesman.[21]

Yet Hamilton had his weaknesses. While some contemporaries adored him, others hated him. His better intentions were at times tainted by arrogance and ambition. As well, his better judgment was at times overtaken by temptation.

His long, complicated, and humiliating affair with Maria Reynolds reveal this weakness. The saga began when the young Mrs. Reynolds appeared on

---

21. Morse, "Alexander Hamilton," p. 22.

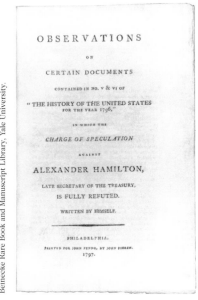

OBSERVATIONS

ON

CERTAIN DOCUMENTS

CONTAINED IN NO. V & VI OF

" THE HISTORY OF THE UNITED STATES
FOR THE YEAR 1796,"

IN WHICH THE

CHARGE OF SPECULATION

AGAINST

ALEXANDER HAMILTON,

LATE SECRETARY OF THE TREASURY,

IS FULLY REFUTED.

WRITTEN BY HIMSELF.

PHILADELPHIA:
PRINTED FOR JOHN FENNO, BY JOHN BIOREN,
1797.

The 1797 title page of Hamilton's defense against charges of misappropriation of government funds in collusion with the shady James Reynolds. Denying the charges Hamilton wrote, "My real crime is an amorous connection with his wife."

Hamilton's Philadelphia doorstep in 1791 to seek his aid. Her story of being abandoned by her husband and left penniless with a five-year-old child was carefully aimed, for Hamilton had a reputation for "benevolence and Humanity to the distress'd." A sordid course of infidelity followed for several years. Hamilton was by no means a smooth operator, as his newness to such an ordeal was "painfully evident in the clumsiness with which he handled the affair."[22]

Rumors of the scandal turned into vicious speculations that Hamilton was using Treasury Department dollars and information to aid alleged schemes connected to Maria's "unsavory" husband, James Reynolds. His rivals, Jefferson and Madison in particular, milked the precarious situation for all its political advantages. The accusations of corruption in his public life seared his reputation like burning coals, threatening his effectiveness as a public servant.[23] During the summer of 1797, he faced the music. In a published pamphlet he defended himself against the false speculations with the fierce reason and skill he had used in so many essays. Then he fully and exhaustively admitted to the affair, making no excuses for himself. "The charge against me," he wrote "is a connection with one James Reynolds for purposes of improper pecuniary speculation. My real crime is an amorous connection with his wife."[24]

However well he handled the situation in the end, the Reynolds affair constituted no minor blemish on Hamilton's character. The colossus of public and political life was himself shown to be a captive of the passions of depravity. The mark did not destroy him, but it hurt, coloring memories of him to this day.

---

22. As quoted in McDonald, *Alexander Hamilton*, pp. 228–229.

23. For Hamilton, his greatest personal calling was that of public service; he refused to jeopardize this, even at the expense of private embarrassment. Richard Brookhiser explains: "Hamilton considered corruption a 'more heinous charge' against a public servant than adultery," Brookhiser, *Alexander Hamilton*, p. 134.

24. Brookhiser, *Alexander Hamilton*, p. 133.

6

PAINED BY ATHEISM, GRIEVED BY TRAGEDY

Scarred from his sins and finished with official cabinet duties, the "Little Lion" toyed with a change of direction. He had made arrangements to move Betsey and the children from Philadelphia to New York, where he could devote himself to the legal profession and to supporting his family. He had some ground to regain on the home front: Betsey had endured the public humiliation of her husband's affair and wanted him home. The children (six and counting) enjoyed his love and attention when he managed to get home between public duties, but needed more time with their father. He needed to educate a new son, to build a new house, and to generate a livelihood.

The story is often told of the time of the exiled French Foreign Minister Talleyrand passed by Hamilton's law office late one night only to glimpse him working away by candlelight. Stunned by the sight, Talleyrand wrote: "I have just come from viewing a man who had made the fortune of his country, but now is working all night in order to support his family."[1] At home he followed a strict program affording him time for the family as well as personal study, writing, and political correspondence. Ever the student,

> he ministered to an insatiable mind. Never tiring of the classics, he kept pace with the printing press. . . . Thus the 'Wealth of Nations' was in his hands as soon after its appearance as a boat could cross the sea. His manner of study was intensive. . . . Walking the floor while reading and studying, it was a comment of his friends that with equal exertion he could have walked from one end of the country to the other.[2]

---

1. Brookhiser, *Alexander Hamilton*, p. 121.
2. As quoted in John C. Hamilton, *The Life of Alexander Hamilton*, p. 10.

Picturing the children shamelessly mimicking their eccentric father as he marched around the house is easy—they might have even heard about how he obtained the habit back in his King's College days before they, or the nation, were born.

Between the demands of his desk work and time with the family, the statesman father was in a season of life where another old habit from his college days was resurfacing—that of his religious devotion. If in previous years a feverish pace of political and professional activities "gave him little time to meditate on religion" in any formal sense, a new cultural urgency and personal watershed brought the Christian faith to the forefront of his concerns.[3]

The great spur to this reawakening of faith was the French Revolution. Like the American war for independence, the revolution in France was a political upheaval, but the similarities ended there. In France, the revolution was an ideological eruption of destructive proportions. Jean Jacques Rousseau's aggressive social-contract philosophy had stoked a revolutionary fire that sought to purge society of traditional beliefs. Atheism was the new religion and Liberty, Equality, and Fraternity became ideological idols for revolutionaries obsessed with the rights of man. Maximilien de Robespierre personified the "bloodthirsty atheistic mob" and was the leader of the Jacobin Club, a group that ironically took the name of a French religious order. The Dutch statesman and theologian, Abraham Kuyper, later spoke to the historical significance of the revolution:

> The French Revolution ignores God. It opposes God. It refuses to recognize a deeper ground of political life than that which is found in nature, that is, in this instance, in man himself. . . . The sovereign God is dethroned and man with his free will is placed in the vacant seat. It is the will of man which determines all things. All power, all authority proceeds from man. . . . It is a sovereignty of the people therefore, which is perfectly identical with atheism.[4]

Hamilton would have agreed. Like Edmund Burke, the great critic of the French Revolution, he was outraged at such revolutionary excesses. Some American leaders favored what they thought to be a revolution inspired by their own, but Hamilton believed "the French Revolution to be no more akin to the American Revolution than the faithless wife in a French novel is like

---

3. Bowers, *Jefferson and Hamilton*, p. 41.

4. Abraham Kuyper, *Lectures on Calvinism* (Grand Rapids: Eerdmans, 1994), pp. 87–88.

the Puritan matron in New England."[5] For him it was an atheistic wrecking ball crashing through the foundations of Christianity. He wrote in 1794:

> Facts, numerous and unequivocal, demonstrate that the present [era] is among the most extraordinary, which have occurred in the history of human affairs. . . . Irreligion, no longer confined to the closets of conceiled sophists, nor to the haunts of wealthy riot, has more or less displayed its hideous front among all classes. . . . Religion and Government have both been stigmatised as abuses; as unwarrantable restraints upon the freedom of man.[6]

One wonders if Hamilton recalled his readings from Plutarch and his observation, jotted in his old army pay book, that religion is the key to civilized society. In the French Revolution he saw the antithesis in action. As years passed he grew all the more alarmed. Wanting the public to understand the severity of the situation, he published a series of essays in 1798 titled *The Stand*. Writing from New York, he declared:

> In reviewing the disgusting spectacle of the French revolution, it is difficult to avert the eye from those features of it which betray a plan to disorganize the human mind itself, as well as to undermine the venerable pillars that support the edifice of civilized society. The attempt by the rulers of a nation to destroy all religious opinion, and to pervert a whole people to Atheism, is a phenomenon of profligacy reserved to consummate the infamy of the unprincipled reformers of France. The proofs of this terrible design are numerous and convincing. . . . The open profession of Atheism in the Convention, received with acclamations; the honorable mention on its journals of a book professing to prove the nothingness of all religion; the institution of a festival to offer public worship to a courtezan decorated with the pompous [title] of "Goddess of Reason;" the congratulatory reception of impious children appearing in the hall of the Convention to lisp blasphemy against the King of Kings; are among the dreadful proofs of a conspiracy to establish Atheism on the ruins of Christianity—to deprive mankind of its best consolations and most animating hopes—and to make a gloomy desert of the universe.[7]

---

5. Ibid., p. 88.

6. *Hamilton Papers*, 27:738–739.

7. Ibid., 31:403.

Similar passages are found in his essays and letters of the time. "His youthful faith had never entirely departed him," writes Forrest McDonald, "and the overt atheism of the French Revolution had rekindled his sense of the importance of religion."[8] The French were ejecting Christianity from the public square. This mattered to Hamilton; it violated the core principles he outlined for himself, for humanity, and for government. America, he feared, was edging dangerously close to the path of the same wrecking ball.

At the close of the eighteenth century, America was already in a spiritual slump of her own. The decade following the American Revolution was, one observer remarked, "the period of the lowest ebb tide of vitality in the history of American Christianity." By 1801 the country's western frontier, led by Baptists and Methodists, would be ablaze with revival, but for now the eastern seaboard, with its Congregational and Episcopal establishments, was sapped of religious fervor. In Virginia, Bishop James Madison announced that the Episcopal church was "too far gone ever to be revived."[9] Further north, Aaron Burr, Hamilton's famous rival, spent a year studying for the ministry before calling it quits and owning up to his own lack of faith. "His reaction," says historian Thomas Fleming of Burr, "was typical of a general decline in theological fervor throughout America. The French Revolution's assault on religion as the bulwark of the ruling class accelerated this trend." The state of things at Yale University also bore witness to the times: Of the Yale graduates in 1796, only *one* claimed to believe in God.[10]

All of this made for an ideologically vulnerable America, and Hamilton knew it. He, along with Federalist Party leaders, feared that French Jacobin influences would take hold and devastate the nation's pivotal (though slumbering) faith consensus, the public order, and even the Constitution.

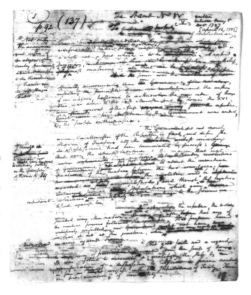

The 1798 manuscript of The Stand, Hamilton's defense of "Christian civilization" against the atheist tempers of the French Revolution.

---

8. McDonald, *Alexander Hamilton*, p. 356.

9. Robert Wallace, "The Rugged Basis of American Protestantism," *Life*, December 26, 1955, p. 72.

10. Thomas Fleming, *Duel: Alexander Hamilton, Aaron Burr and the Future of America* (New York: Basic Books, 1999), pp. 80–81.

Francophiles such as Thomas Jefferson and Tom Paine were seen as potential arms of the Jacobin threat. In a letter to Timothy Pickering, Hamilton even proposed a day of "humiliation and prayer." He noted, "It is far from evident to me that the progress of the war may not call on us to defend our fire sides & our altars. And any plan which does not look forward to this as soon as possible will in my opinion be a superficial one." He had warned years earlier, "Symptoms of the too great prevalence of this [French] system in the United States are alarmingly visible," and wrote in 1798:

> France, swelled to a gigantic size and aping ancient Rome, except in her virtues, plainly meditates the controul of mankind, and is actually giving law to nations. Unless they quickly rouse and compel her to abdicate her insolent claim, they will verify the truth of that philosophy.[11]

He felt the nearness of the threat and feared its force over a complacent people.

Ever mindful of the public good, Hamilton sought all possible means to express the view that Christianity was imperative to the aims of the United States. No example illustrates this point better than George Washington's Farewell Address, delivered via publication in the press on September 19, 1796. Hamilton, who had frequently written many letters and speeches on Washington's behalf, was its main author. During the previous spring, Washington requested his aid in the task of drawing up a draft, hoping "that the whole may appear in a plain style; and be handed to the public in an honest, unaffected, simple garb." Political disputes of the day, domestic and abroad, provided much material to cover, and Hamilton addressed them with the precision and eloquence

President Washington's Farewell Address. He delivered this noted address, ghostwritten by Hamilton, in Philadelphia on September 17, 1796.

---

11. *Hamilton Papers*, 20:545; 26:740; 21:408.

called for by the moment. What resulted was a work that decisively faced the concerns of the times. Moreover, it conveyed the deeper sentiments and principles that the public could, together with their first president, hold as the prized possessions of a great and just nation. As one writer explains, "The growing pains of government, the antagonisms of parties, sectional interests, tax burdens, overseas affinities, and the menaces and blandishments of warring foreign powers were the lava of which the Address was compounded. But, veiled by the dignity of their style, the immediate controversies faded from the memories of later generations, leaving only the proverb, not the parable."[12] Within this "proverb," Hamilton took pains to underscore the principles that mattered most:

> Of all the dispositions and habits which lead to political prosperity, Religion and morality are indispensable supports. In vain would that man claim the tribute of Patriotism, who should labour to subvert these great Pillars of human happiness, these firmest props of the duties of Men and citizens. The mere Politician, equally with the pious man ought to respect and to cherish them. A volume could not trace all their connections with private and public felicity. Let it simply be asked where is the security for prosperity, for reputation, for life, if the sense of religious obligation *desert* the oaths, which are the instruments of investigation in Courts of Justice? And let us with caution indulge the supposition, that morality can be maintained without religion. Whatever may be conceded to the influence of refined education on minds of peculiar structure, reason and experience both forbid us to expect that National morality can prevail in exclusion of religious principle.[13]

As the voice of President Washington, the colossus cemented religion and morality as first things for the nation. He had ended the paragraph in a previous draft with the question: "Does [national morality] not require

---

12. Robert Hendrickson, *Hamilton II* (New York: Mason Charter, 1976) pp. 366, 370. James C. Humes further explains: "Hamilton saw the opportunity of writing the political equivalent of a last will and testament. For the Father of his Country, the lawyer Hamilton would execute a document that would stipulate the principles for protecting the constitutional framework of the governmental and preserving the political estate of the nation," James C. Humes, *My Fellow Americans* (New York: Praeger, 1992), p. 7.

13. John C. Fitzpatrick, ed., *George Washington—Original Manuscript Sources* (Washington: Government Printing Office, 1940), 35:229.

the aid of a generally received and divinely authoritative religion?"[14] Making no scholastic appeal to natural law, civil religion, or the covenantal roots of federalism, he appraised the realities of the young nation and sought to affirm those values that are vital.

At home, Hamilton continued to work through his worries for the nation—and made plans for a garden.

The Grange located on Kingsbridge Road in New York City, the residence of Alexander and Elizabeth Hamilton.

America's political future looked bleak, and he desired more of the quiet and deep joys of family life. Also, much reflection was needed. If faith was, as he believed, so imperative to the nation, how then should it bear on his own life? The Christian habits he had learned as a boy and practiced through his life answered the question for him. His son, John C. Hamilton, recalled how his father "sought relief from the painful reflections which the growing delusion of the country forced upon him, in the duties of religion, in the circle of domestic joys, and in the embellishment of his rural retreat."[15] Soon enough, however, Hamilton's life was invaded by another watershed event—this time a personal tragedy.

The eldest of the Hamilton children, Philip, was a nineteen-year-old graduate of Columbia University, formerly King's College. As he was studying law under his father's guidance at the Grange, the newly built New York estate, Philip appeared most likely to follow in Hamilton's footsteps. In a tragic irony, however, the father would end up following in the son's.

On a November evening in 1801, Philip joined a friend for an evening at a New York theater. There they spotted George Eacker, a prominent Republican lawyer who had, several months earlier, given a speech that

---

14. F. Ernest Johnson, ed., *Wellsprings of the American Spirit* (New York: Cooper Square Publishers, 1964), p. 57; In "The Stand No. III" (April 1798) Hamilton parenthetically argues that morality is interwoven with religion: "and morality *must* fall with religion," *Hamilton Papers*, 21:405.

15. As quoted in Hendrickson, *Hamilton II*, p. 556. Hamilton wrote to his wife in 1801: "Indeed my Eliza, you are very essential to me. Your virtues more and more endear you to me and experience more and more convinces me that true happiness is only to be found in the bosom of one's own family," Fleming, *Duel*, p. 12.

threw a polemical jab at Hamilton, accusing him of wanting to use the army to suppress Republicans.[16] Philip still smarted from the assault on his father and accosted Eacker. The argument continued at a nearby tavern following the show. Eacker declared that he was offended by the youth, and Philip showed no interest in apologizing. Honor was at stake and, as was the custom, a duel was scheduled.

When Hamilton the elder learned of the situation, he "commanded his Son, when on the ground, to reserve his fire 'till after Mr. E, had shot and then to discharge his pistol in the air." Chances of missing were good, and Hamilton's advice directed Philip to aim at honor and grace rather than pride and vengeance. The two duelists met each other at a New Jersey field on November 23. Eacker's shot struck Philip above the right hip, mortally wounding him. He was rushed to the home of his uncle, John Church, where his mother and father soon found him. The scene was one of immense grief: "After twenty-four hours of agony, with his father lying, weeping, on one side of the bed with him and with his mother on the other, Philip died."[17]

Mother and father were devastated. To add to their sorrows, their oldest daughter, Angelica, fell into a depressed and irrational state, and for the rest of her life she would speak of Philip as though he were alive. Letters from friends came pouring in, but it was four months before Hamilton could bring himself to respond. Benjamin Rush offered spiritual support from Philadelphia:

> Permit a whole family to mingle their tears with yours upon the late distressing event that has taken place in your family. . . . Many, many tears have been Shed in our city upon your Account. . . . God does not judge, nor condemn like man. There are no limits to his mercy.[18]

From Charleston, Charles Pinckney wrote: "I am much afflicted at the event, and most sincerely condole with Mrs. Hamilton & yourself on a misfortune which only religion & time can alleviate."[19]

---

16. Brookhiser, *Alexander Hamilton*, p. 198.

17. As quoted in McDonald, *Alexander Hamilton*, p. 356. One of Philip's Columbia classmates described the scene: "On a Bed without curtains lay poor Phil, pale and languid, his rolling, distorted eyeballs darting forth the flashes of delirium—on one side of him on the same bed—lay his agonized father—on the other his distracted mother. . . . Returning Home I quickened my pace almost unconsciously, hoping to escape the image as well as the reality of what I had witnessed!" Brookhiser, *Alexander Hamilton*, p. 199.

18. *Hamilton Papers*, 25:435.

19. Ibid., 25:469.

From London came Rufus King's encouraging words:

> Both as a friend and a father I do most unfeignibly participate and condole with you in the heavy affliction that has fallen upon your family. It would be altogether vain for me to have recourse to the usual Topics of consolation, in so severe a Calamity: it must be sought for among the treasures of your own Mind, which nature has so eminently endowed; and after a while, it will likewise be found in the promising Branches of your family, which remain to recall to your remembrance, as well as to console you for, the loss you have suffered.[20]

Portrait by Ezra Ames, Circa 1800-1801, Fleming, Thomas. Alexander Hamilton, Aaron Burr and the Future of America. Basic Books: NY, 1999 (p. 240).

A late portrait of Hamilton by Ezra Ames. Grief and perhaps even depression are visible after his fall from political power and amid family tragedy.

In his March reply to Benjamin Rush, Hamilton shared that the event was "beyond comparison the most afflicting of my life." He reflected:

> My loss is indeed great. The highest as well as the eldest hope of my family has been taken from me. . . . But why should I repine? It was the will of heaven; and he is now out of the reach of the seductions and calamities of a world, full of folly, full of vice, full of danger—of least value in proportion as it is best known. I firmly trust also that he has safely reached the haven of eternal repose and felicity.[21]

The father would never fully recover from his son's death, but after four months under the weight of oppressive grief, Hamilton's words convey an emerging peace. He was a different man than he had been when he stormed the British redoubt, when he took his oath as treasury secretary, and when he succumbed to the temptations of Maria Reynolds. Bruised and broken

---

20. Ibid., 25:498.

21. Ibid., 25:583–584.

by losses public and private, he was seasoned by the "seductions and calamities" of his world.

7

A Christian Strategy?

If the French Revolution roused the piety of Hamilton's youth, Philip's death drove the substance of faith back into his heart. His wife remained devout as ever; some called her "the little Saint."[1] Still missing from Hamilton's own devotion, however, was any formal church membership. This hesitancy, historians suppose, stemmed from the competing loyalties between Episcopalians and Presbyterians. Both traditions left considerable marks on his life, but he was unwilling to wed his identity to one and not the other. Hamilton drew on each tradition to inspire his increasing devotion and creative activism.

Increasingly disturbed by the state of American political affairs, he was unable to enjoy a quiet and contemplative spring at the Grange. Thomas Jefferson was at the nation's helm, and Aaron Burr—bitter that the presidency was not his own—made for a feisty vice president. The influence of the Republican Party was, by all Federalist counts, spoiling America. Following Jefferson's election, the *Boston Centinel* mockingly announced the death of Hamilton's party. In the lion's den of New York politics, every Federalist candidate for the State Assembly was defeated. Robert Troup wrote to Rufus King of their mutual friend's mood following the election:

> Hamilton is supremely disgusted with the state of our political affairs. He has all along said and still maintains the opinion that Jefferson and his party had not talents or virtues sufficient to administer the government well; and he entertains no doubt that they will finally ruin our affairs and plunge us into serious

---

1. Hendrickson, *The Rise and Fall of Alexander Hamilton*, p. 546. Of Hamilton, Forrest McDonald writes: "Now, in the wake of Philip's death, he became as devout as he had been as a protégé of the Reverend Hugh Knox," McDonald, *Alexander Hamilton*, p. 356.

commotions. Although he does not think this result will immediately take place, yet he predicts it is not so remote as many might imagine. He assures me that nothing short of a general convulsion will again call him into public life.[2]

When Jefferson began planning to repeal the Judiciary Act (passed by a Federalist Congress a year earlier), Hamilton started making public appearances. The repeal would sweep away judicial posts that Adams had filled with Federalists, and most enraging to Hamilton, would threaten the independence of the judiciary. His largest worry, however, remained the so-called Jacobin threat: "Atheism and the absence of religion in public polity filled Hamilton with unfeigned horror."[3] Were his "indispensable supports" for America going to be ruthlessly flung aside as in France? Allan McLane Hamilton wrote of his grandfather:

> To him the growing influence of the "Jacobins" and their party meant only ruin and disaster, and though he, perhaps, did not fully share Horace Binney's later expressed sentiment that he 'believed Jefferson was the full incarnation of Satan,' he had good reason to dread the influence of a man and his supporters who had done so much to weaken the respect for the Constitution of the United States.[4]

While some members of the "late"

Vice President Aaron Burr Jr., grandson of New England theologian Jonathan Edwards and student of the renowned John Witherspoon, president of the College of New Jersey. An orphan raised by his clergyman uncle, the Reverend Jonathan Edwards Jr., Burr became notorious for his ambition and waywardness. Washington and Jefferson distrusted him. His infamy grew as his political prospects declined when he felled Hamilton in a duel.

---

2. *Hamilton Papers*, 26:376.

3. Hendrickson, *The Rise and Fall of Hamilton*, p. 546.

4. Allan McLane Hamilton, *The Intimate Life of Alexander Hamilton* (London: Duckworth, 1910), p. 335.

Alexander Hamilton

Federalist party began to murmur about seceding from the Union to start their own New England confederacy, Hamilton (who opposed such fancies) was up against questions of personal identity. He confided in longtime friend Gouverneur Morris:

> Mine is an odd destiny. Perhaps no man in the U[nited] States has sacrificed or done more for the present Constitution than myself— and contrary to all my anticipations of its fate, as you know from the very beginning I am still labouring to prop the frail and worthless fabric. Yet I have the murmurs of its friends no less than the curses of its foes for my reward. What can I do better than withdraw from the Scene? Every day proves to me more and more that this American world was not made for me.[5]

All the avenues of his depression, disenchantment, conviction, work, and faith converged at this awkward intersection. Was he, after all, truly an American? The nation was fast becoming a world far different than that for which Hamilton had studied, fought, written, argued, led, and prayed. Were his colossal efforts all in vain? At this crossroads, he would be forced to choose a path, one of which meant a withdraw from the public square.

Federalist Party leader James A. Bayard of Delaware.

What had been the calling and vocation of his life, however, was still in his blood. He could not ignore it. Less than two months after sharing his lament with Morris, Hamilton was brewing a new idea. His inspiration came when James A. Bayard, a key Federalist leader from Delaware, requested his advice on reinvigorating party strategy. Hamilton responded with a letter outlining carefully thought-out plans for what he called the Christian Constitutional Society. "I am glad to find that it is in contemplation to adopt a plan of conduct," he wrote Bayard. By way of introduction he explained:

---

5. Kline, ed., *Alexander Hamilton*, p. 389.

Park Row and St. Paul's Chapel in New York circa 1798.

I will comply with your invitation by submitting some ideas which from time to time have passed through my mind. Nothing is more fallacious than to expect to produce any valuable or permanent results, in political projects, by relying merely on the reason of men. Men are rather reasoning tha[n] reasonable animals for the most part governed by the impulse of passion. . . . Unluckily however for us in the competition for the passions of the people our opponents have great advantages over us; for the plain reason, that the vicious are far more active than the good passions, and that to win the latter to our side we must renounce our principles & our objects, & unite in corrupting public opinion till it becomes fit for nothing but mischief. . . . In my opinion the present Constitution is the standard to which we are to cling. Under its banners, *bona fide* must we combat our political foes.[6]

---

6. *Hamilton Papers*, 25:606.

Alexander Hamilton

The groundwork laid, he then set forth the details of his plan. The objects for the society would be: "1st the support of the Christian Religion" and "2nd the support of the Constitution of the United States." A central "directing council" would be organized to oversee state "sub-directing" councils with their own local societies. As to the nuts and bolts of how it would operate, there would be three main "means." First, councils would distribute information: "It is essential to be able to disseminate *gratis* useful publications" via newspapers, pamphlets, and so on. Second, the groups would use "all lawful means" to campaign for the election of "fit men" into political office. Third, the societies would work together for promoting charitable institutions in the country's growing cities for "the relief of Emigrants" and "Academies each with one professor for instructing the different Classes of Mechanics & Elements of Chemistry." On this final idea, Hamilton took pains to mention that "the cities have been employed by the Jacobins to give an impulse to the country."[7]

He was thinking politically, constitutionally, socially, and religiously all at the same time. It was a grassroots strategy with a federal organization combining the best of religious and political disciplines. If Jefferson and his Jacobin brood were going to win America with their appeal to passions, Hamilton would match them and beat them by permeating society with Christian virtues and constitutional allegiances. The Federalist Party's need for a better strategy offered Hamilton an opportunity to bring the nation back to the road of regeneration. It was good for America and good for the Federalist Party—always a winning combination in the mind of the colossus.

Alas, Bayard was unconvinced. He replied that such "clubs" would only "revive a thousand jealousies and suspicions which now begin to slumber"; he felt it best to let the Democratic-Republicans defeat themselves. Hamilton let the issue be and focused his energies on practicing law. Some New England faithful, however, still feared the "infidel" in Washington and the dire events that might lie ahead. They might have appreciated the society. The story is told that a few northern farmers, fearing the onslaught of an American version of the French Revolution, hung Bibles down wells and oiled up their flintlocks.[8] These exceptions aside, the influence of fervent and Federalist New England clergy was giving way to Jefferson's growing popularity, and still more dark clouds hovered over Hamilton's destiny.

---

7. Ibid.

8. Hendrickson, *The Rise and Fall of Hamilton*, p. 550.

8

A MORTAL WOUND

At Christmas that year, Hamilton sent an update to his friend Charles Pinckney. "A garden," he wrote "is a very usual refuge of a disappointed politician." He noted that English melons are thought to be "very fine" and asked his friend if he might "send me some seed both of the Water & Muss Melons?" In passing, he offered Pinckney a taste of his disappointment with America's political scene: "The last *lullaby* message [Jefferson's message to Congress], instead of inspiring contempt, attracts praise. Mankind are forever destined to be the dupes of bold & cunning imposture."[1] Enough of his energies had gone to grooming the public square; if the public was content to see the nation overrun by weeds, so be it. Hamilton needed new seeds to sow, and melons were the order of the day.

He enjoyed a quiet winter attending to work projects at his home, the Grange, and the needs of his growing children. Past years held a storehouse of painful memories for the family, but the previous summer brought the joys of a new little boy into the fold. They named him Philip. When Betsey was out of town visiting family, Hamilton wrote to her:

> I am here my beloved Betsey with my two little boys. . . who will be my bedfellows to night. The day I have passed was agreeable as it could be in your absence; but you need not be told how much difference your presence would have made. Things are now going on here pretty briskly. I am making some innovations which I am sure you will approve.
>
> The remainder of the Children were well yesterday. Eliza pouts and plays, and displays more and more her ample stock of Caprice.[2]

---

1. Kline, ed., *Alexander Hamilton*, p. 392.

2. Ibid., pp. 392–393.

One of his innovations for the family garden was to plant thirteen gum trees in a circle on the lawn. He may have been displaying a little caprice himself, but the colonial tribute was unfortunately short-lived as the clustered trees failed to take.

His legal skills continued to win bread for the family and acclaim from peers. In February 1804, he argued a case to the New York Court of Electors regarding a Federalist printer named Harry Croswell who had been indicted for libel. Contending that the *truth* of a publication must serve as a defense against such a charge and that juries must consider the truth or falsehood of such statements, he "presented some of the most important arguments on the law of libel and the freedom of the press heard in an American courtroom in the early nineteenth century." One judge recalled that Hamilton's "whole soul, was enlisted in the cause."[3] Other displays of reason and principle affirmed Hamilton's top place in the legal field.

Still, Hamilton was haunted by things political. For years he had opposed Aaron Burr's political ambitions and liked him even less than Jefferson. In doing so, he cultivated a determined enemy. Burr, Hamilton thought, was a fair-weather Federalist with few principles apart from personal ambition. Hamilton, in turn, was the ruthless thorn in Burr's flesh. The sentiments were magnified when New York Governor George Clinton declined another term and Burr, still vice president but looking to make a move to local politics, vied for the Federalist backing. Hamilton threw his weight behind a Democratic-Republican candidate named Lansing (who would later refuse the nomination) and acted as the "self-appointed chief of the anti-Burr movement."[4] He waged the latter campaign discreetly, but effectively; Burr was defeated.

Things grew ugly when Burr caught wind of what his nemesis had been up to and was shown a report of remarks Hamilton allegedly made criticizing his character. He could take no more. A series of angry letters were exchanged demanding explanations and apologies, and Burr made it clear that the quarrel was now a matter of honor. On the evening of June 27, 1804, Hamilton received Burr's official challenge to a duel that would "vindicate that honor at such hazard as the nature of the case demands."[5]

Like his son before him, the father's destiny fell into the hands of what

---

3. Ibid., p. 394. Richard Morris further comments: "His incisive mind and massive legal erudition, assimilated with phenomena rapidity, were quickly recognized, and as attorney and counselor at law he was *primus inter pares*," Morris, *Witnesses at the Creation*, p. 40.

4. Kline, ed., *Alexander Hamilton*, p. 396.

5. Ibid., p. 400.

was in his time a gentleman's code of honor. No man, when challenged to a duel, could in good conscience decline, even though common law held that deaths in duels were murders. In many cases the "interviews," as they were called, were carefully arranged; pistols were fired and both men walked away with honor intact. Nevertheless, as the date and time for the duel were being set, Hamilton went through the eerie motions of a man preparing to die. He completed as much legal work as he could, arranged his estate, named executors, and drew up his will. Hamilton attended to all this with his usual diligent efficiency in matters of business. He was far less practiced in arranging for closure to his personal life.

How does a man reckon with the possibility of death? Perhaps he had pondered the question years before on the battlefield, but the assurance of dying a hero's death would be no comfort to him in a duel. (Duels were hidden and private events where men settled scores; a gentleman's code dictated their existence but the publicly spoken view was that death by duel was a shameful death.) Hamilton himself had publicly condemned duels— he had lost his own son to one. The ironies must have weighed on him.

Betsey and the seven children had no knowledge of what was happening. Hamilton thought of them deeply and dearly, wondering if by grim fate he might not have another summer with them. On July 4, one week before the duel, he penned a letter to be given to his wife in the event of his death.

This letter, my very dear Eliza, will not be delivered to you, unless I shall first have terminated my earthly career; to begin, as I humbly hope from redeeming grace and divine mercy, a happy immortality.

If it had been possible for me to have avoided the interview, my love for you and my precious children would have been alone a decisive motive. But it was not possible, without sacrifices which would have rendered me unworthy of your esteem. I need not tell you of the pangs I feel, from the idea of quitting you and exposing you to the anguish which I know you would feel. Nor could I dwell on the topic lest it should unman me.

The consolations of Religion, my beloved, can alone support you; and these you have a right to enjoy. Fly to the bosom of your God and be comforted. With my last idea; I shall cherish the sweet hope of meeting you in a better world.

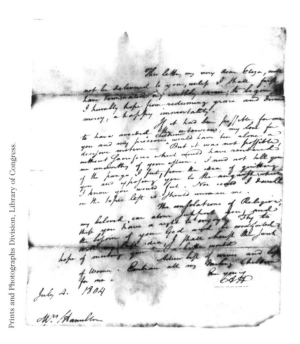

*Hamilton's last letter to his wife, dated July 4,
1804, to be delivered upon his death.*

Adieu best of wives and best of Women.
Embrace all my darling Children for me.[6]

As a man who had spent much of his life
harnessing the power of words, he knew
that brevity could best convey vast
meaning. It would not have been an easy
letter to write or read.

Hamilton also appreciated the value
of words for the judgment of posterity
and thus drew up a personal apologetic.
His "Statement on Impending Duel with
Aaron Burr" outlined his reasons for
fighting the duel (though not desiring
it), his understanding of Burr's concerns, and what his strategy would be
when the dreaded event commenced.
He began:

On my expected interview with Col
Burr, I think it proper to make some
remarks explanatory of my conduct, motives and views.

I am certainly desirous of avoiding this interview, for the most
cogent of reasons.

1. My religious and moral principles are strongly opposed to the
   practice of Duelling, and it would even give me pain to be obliged
   to shed the blood of a fellow creature in a private combat
   forbidden by the laws.

2. My wife and Children are extremely dear to me, and my life is of
   the utmost importance to them, in various views.

3. I feel a sense of obligation towards my creditors. . . .

4. I am conscious of no *ill-will* to Col Burr, distinct from political

---

6. *Hamilton Papers*, 26:293.

opposition, which, as I trust, has proceeded from pure and upright motives.[7]

Regarding Burr's claims, he went on:

> It is not my design, by what I have said to affix any odium on the conduct of Col Burr, in this case. . . . He may have supposed himself under a necessity of acting as he has done. . . . I trust, at the same time, that the world will do me the Justice to believe, that I have not censured him on any light grounds, or from unworthy inducements. . . . It is also my ardent wish that I may have been more mistaken than I think I have been, and that he by his future conduct may shew himself worthy of all confidence and esteem, and prove an ornament and blessing to his Country.[8]

As to the event itself, Hamilton noted his plans to do that which he had advised Philip to do in his duel with Eacker:

> I have resolved, if our interview is conducted in the usual manner, and it pleases God to give me the opportunity, to *reserve* and *throw away* my first fire, and *I have thoughts* even of *reserving* my second fire— and thus giving a double opportunity to Col Burr to pause and reflect.[9]

In a second letter for delivery to Betsey, he explained the final point:

> The scruples of a Christian have determined me to expose my own life to any extent rather than subject myself to the guilt of taking the life of another. This must increase my hazards and redoubles my pangs for you. But you had rather I should die innocent than live guilty.[10]

There was no mention of their son's death by similar designs, but Hamilton the father surely felt some burden honorably to do as he had advised his own boy to do. He concluded:

> Heaven can preserve me and I humbly hope will but in the contrary

---

7. Ibid., 26:278–280.
8. Ibid.
9. Ibid.
10. Ibid., 26:307–308.

event, I charge you to remember that you are a Christian. God's will be done. The will of a merciful God must be good. Once more Adieu My Darling Wife.[11]

His words reflected a growing, even resolved, sense of the inevitable. One historian describes this as "a sense of fitness, an eloquent melancholy, a feeling of mystery and of a work unfinished."[12]

The last few years had taught him to savor things most dear and meaningful; during his final days on the Grange he embraced his family as a loving leader and tender father. As Sundays were a day of family worship, Hamilton led Betsey and the children through the Episcopal prayer-book service on the final Sunday before the duel. He prayed aloud:

> O God, who knowest the weakness and corruption of our nature, and the manifold temptations we daily meet with . . . have compassion on our infirmities . . . that we may be effectually restrained from sin, and excited to duty.

Brief and honest, the prayer conveyed the posture of his heart. It also fit the charge of his life—to be rightly restrained and excited to duty. That same night Hamilton desired the company of his son, thirteen-year-old John Church Hamilton. John later recalled:

A monument marks the site of the duel between Aaron Burr Jr. and Hamilton at Weehawken, New Jersey, on the west bank of the Hudson River.

I was sitting in a room at The Grange when at a slight noise I turned and saw my father in the doorway standing silently looking at me with a most sweet and beautiful expression of countenance, full of tenderness, and without any of the preoccupations of business he sometimes had.

"John," said he, "won't you come and sleep with me tonight," and his voice was frank as if it had been my

---

11. Ibid.

12. Hendrickson, *The Rise and Fall of Hamilton*, p. 645.

brother's instead of my father's. . . . In the morning very early he awakened me. Taking my hands in his palms, all four hands extended, he told me to repeat The Lord's Prayer.[13]

Early in the morning a few days later, Hamilton slipped out of the house and headed for the dueling ground. Betsey and the children had no idea what grief the day would bring.

At Weehawken, New Jersey, on the Hudson's west bank, was an isolated patch of land overlooking the river. It was a grassy spot, shouldered by cliffs and banked on one end by a granite boulder and a large cedar tree. The remoteness of the place made it a popular spot for duelists. Philip Hamilton had gone to his death in the same area. The "Seconds," William Van Ness for Burr and Nathaniel Pendleton for Hamilton, had agreed upon the specifications for the deadly business, and Hamilton's family physician, David Hosack, was on hand should his services be necessary. The duelists faced each other at a distance of ten paces, or roughly twenty feet. The pistols were of English make with nine-inch barrels and were .544 caliber; as fate would have it, they were the exact pair used by Philip and Eacker. With weapons ready, everything was set in place.

Hamilton's unusual strategy was also still in place. He privately told Pendleton that "he had made up his mind not to fire at Colonel Burr the first time, but to receive his fire, and fire in the air." Pendleton urged him not to be so charitable, but Hamilton persisted, "It is the effect of a religious scruple, and does not admit of reasoning. It is useless to say more on the subject, as my purpose is definitely fixed." Burr, of course, knew nothing of this plan and had intentions of his own.

When "Present!" was called, the men were free to fire as they pleased. According to Pendleton's published account of the duel, Burr fired first. Hamilton's body jerked as the bullet entered his right side. His muscles tightened and his gun fired before he collapsed to the ground. Hosack was called in and found Hamilton "sitting on the ground, supported in the arms of Mr. Pendleton. His countenance of death I shall never forget—He had at that instant just strength to say, 'This is a mortal wound, Doctor,' when he sunk away, and became to all appearances lifeless."[14] Pendleton and Hosack rushed him to a boat and the reviving airs of the river. Hamilton regained consciousness for a moment and warned the men to be careful

---

13. Ibid., pp. 637–638.
14. Ibid., pp. 637–640.

with his pistol which was lying on the boat's floor; not knowing he had fired, he feared it was still loaded. While Burr's shot had landed a mortal wound, Hamilton's had shattered a cedar branch nowhere near Burr.

Hours later at the nearby home of a friend, Hamilton steadied himself and made the urgent request for a visitor. Benjamin Moore was the Episcopal bishop of New York and rector of Trinity Church, where Hamilton worshiped regularly. He was also the president of Columbia College and a friend of Hamilton's. In his account written the following evening (see Appendices), the bishop told of how he approached Hamilton's bed and "with the utmost calmness and composure," Hamilton said:

The duel at Weehawken between Hamilton and Burr, July 11, 1804.

My dear Sir, you perceive my unfortunate situation, and no doubt have been made acquainted with the circum stances which led to it. It is my desire to receive the Communion at your hands. I hope you will not conceive there is any impropriety in my request. . . . It has for some time past been the wish of my heart, and it was my intention to take an early opportunity of uniting myself to the church, by the reception of that holy ordinance.[15]

The request put Moore in a difficult spot. He held that the law of God commanded his absolute condemnation of the practice of dueling, and that he could not overlook that charge even under these circumstances. Moreover, the church was strict in seeing

15. Syrett and Cooke, ed., *Interview in Weehawken*, pp. 144–145.

that so-called conversions truly evidenced spiritual rebirth—a process taking time that Hamilton did not have. Moore offered compassion and support, but had to decline Hamilton's request.

Hamilton then sent for a Presbyterian friend, the Reverend Dr. John M. Mason. Again he requested the holy sacrament; again it was denied. Mason explained that Presbyterian polity did not allow the Lord's Supper to be privately administered. Like Moore, he comforted the dying statesman, then reminded him that Communion is only "an exhibition and pledge of the mercies" of Christ and that those mercies were available to men apart from Communion. Hamilton said he understood but desired the exhibition just the same. Of the duel, he told Mason: "It was always against my principles. I used every expedient to avoid the interview; but I have found for some

Hamilton's friend the Right Reverend Benjamin Moore, Episcopal bishop of New York, rector of Trinity Church, and president of Columbia College.

time past, that my life must be exposed to that man. I went to the field determined not to take his life." Mason later told that while Hamilton was sharing these things with him he paused, clasped his hands toward heaven, and said: "I have a tender reliance on the mercy of the Almighty, through the mercy of the Lord Jesus Christ."[16]

Oliver Wolcott Jr., a young friend of Hamilton's, was present and wrote to his wife: "[Hamilton] suffers great pain—which he endures like a Hero. . . . He has, of late years experienced his conviction of the truths of the Christian Religion, and has desired to receive the Sacrament—but none of the Clergy who have yet been consulted will administer it."[17] Their refusal to grant Hamilton's wish was due to the high loyalties they held to their priestly offices and the guidelines therein. Even in dying, it appeared Hamilton would not find a denominational home.

However, Bishop Moore returned to visit him the following day and spoke further with Hamilton about the duel and the nature of his spiritual

---

16. J. M. Mason, *An Oration Commemorative of the Late Major-General Alexander Hamilton* (London: R. Edwards et al., 1804), p. 26.

17. Hendrickson, *The Rise and Fall of Hamilton*, p. 642.

convictions. "I proceeded to converse with him on the subject of receiving the Communion," wrote Moore, "and told him that with respect to the qualifications of those who wished to become partakers of that holy ordinance, my enquiries could not be made in language more expressive that that which was used by our Church." After posing several questions to Hamilton that amounted to a statement of faith, Moore reported that he "lifted up his hands and said, 'With utmost sincerity of heart I can answer all those questions in the affirmative.'" Hamilton received his Communion with devotion:

> Almighty, everliving God, Maker of Mankind, who dost correct those whom thou dost love, and chastise everyone whom thou dost receive; grant that thy servant recover his bodily health, if it be thy gracious will; and that whensoever his soul shall depart from the body, it may be without spot; through Jesus Christ our Lord. Amen.

Before dying, Hamilton reaffirmed to Moore "a strong confidence in the mercy of God through the intercession of the Redeemer." With the bishop, Hosack, Wolcott, Church, Elizabeth, and the seven children at his side, the statesman "expired without a struggle, and—almost—without a groan."[18]

Dr. Hosack quoted fitting words from the Roman poet Horace:

> *Incorrupta fides, nudaque veritas,*
> *Quando ullum invenient parem?*
> *Multis ille bonis flebilis occidit.*

> When will incorruptible Faith and naked Truth
> Find another his equal?
> He died wept by many.[19]

As word of his death flashed across New England, the public was shaken with grief. Citizen associations quickly convened to draw up resolutions for honoring the fallen general. From town to town it was "Resolved Unanimously" that civic leaders would "unite with their fellow citizens of all classes in every suitable demonstration of sorrow for the death of

---

18. Syrett and Cooke, ed., *Interview in Weehawken*, pp. 144–147.
19. Fleming, *Duel*, p. 331.

Alexander Hamilton

General Alexander Hamilton." Shops were closed, bells were muffled and tolled at intervals, and a sea of black crape ribbons streamed from the sleeves and hats of grieving citizens. The nation had not mourned so deeply since General Washington's death years before. Newspapers carried the news southward and overseas. The *Norfolk Ledger* announced:

> *Let us Mourn!!!*— The good, the wise, the patriotic Alexander Hamilton; whose whole life was devoted to the service of man; from the exercise of whose talents, this country has derived benefits of the most incalculable magnitude. . . . This great and virtuous man, who was the unchanging friend of Washington, died, on Thursday, July 12, 1804.[20]

The *Boston Centinel* ran a copy of a 1798 letter to President Adams in which Washington spoke highly of Hamilton:

> He is enterprising—quick in his perceptions—and his judgment intuitively great: qualities essential to a great military character; and therefore I repeat, that his loss *will be irreparable*.[21]

Even the Democratic-Republican *Charleston Courier* joined the lament:

Mrs. Alexander Hamilton
at eighty-nine years of age in 1846.

> We must consider the death of General Hamilton as the greatest loss, not only which the country has hitherto sustained, but far greater than it is possible for it to sustain at this time, by the death of any single individual. . . . A colossus of might he stood; the American commonwealth on his shoulders; with one foot in the

---

20. William Coleman, *Death of Alexander Hamilton* (Boston and New York: Houghton Mifflin, 1904), pp. 30.

21. Ibid., p. 160.

vigour of manhood, and the other in the counsel of ripened years.[22]

While a few applauded Burr, the outpouring of emotion spoke volumes of Hamilton's stature in the eyes of his countrymen. The laments both grieved his loss and celebrated his greatness; the media of his day left a mighty memorial of the way a nation honors one who so perseveringly honored it.

From pulpits and podiums came sermons and speeches eulogizing the fallen general. Church and community leaders condemned the practice of dueling, then cradled the lost hero with the honor of their words and the exhortations of Scripture. The Honorable Harrison Otis told a Boston audience:

> Indeed the public character of Hamilton, and his measures from this period, are intimately connected with the history of our country, that it is impossible to do justice to one without devoting a volume to the other. . . . The religious fervor of his last moments was not an impulse of decaying nature yielding to its fears, but the result of a firm conviction of the truths of the Gospel. I am well informed, that in early life, the evidences of the Christian religion had attracted his furious examination, and attained his deliberate assent to their truth. . . . And that however their edifying propensities might have yielded occasionally to the business and temptations of life, they always resumed their influences, and would probably have prompted him to a public profession of his faith in his Redeemer.[23]

Otis and others likely feared that Bishop Moore's account of Hamilton's dying moments would become prey for skeptics. Eliphalet Nott urged his Albany congregation:

> He dies a Christian. . . . Let not the sneering infidel persuade you that this last act of homage to the Saviour, resulted from an enfeebled state of mental faculties. . . . No; his opinions concerning the Divine Mission of Jesus Christ, and the validity of the holy scriptures had long been settled. . . . And had his life been spared, it was his determination to have published them to the world, together with the facts and reasons on which they were founded.

22. Ibid., pp. 174–175.

23. Harrison G. Otis, *Eulogy on Gen. Alexander Hamilton*, July 25, 1804 (Boston: Manning & Loring, 1804), pp. 11–20.

He then opened the door for listeners to follow Hamilton's lead:

> How are the mighty fallen! Fallen before the desolating hand of death. . . . The ruins of the tomb are an emblem of the ruins of the world . . . the gospel in the Cross of its great High Priest, offers you all a sanctuary. A sanctuary secure and abiding. . . . Every thing else is fugitive; every thing else is mutable; every thing else will fail you. But this, the citadel of the Christian's hopes, will never fail you.[24]

Nott was ringing the bells both to honor a lost hero and to announce the sacred grace waiting in a risen Lord. He let Hamilton's death be for America what, in many ways, it must be: a journey of redemption.

Did Aaron Burr hear the message? Later in life he evidenced regret for the duel, but was never too far from defending his actions. In a Staten Island hotel room in 1836 he lay ill, his own death imminent. There, this grandson of Jonathan Edwards, America's premier theologian, was visited by a Dutch Reformed clergyman. The minister did not offer Communion; Burr had not requested it. But he did pray for Burr in his final moments. Burr may have outlived his nemesis by thirty-two years, yet his experience with death did not appear as "life-embracing" as it was for Hamilton.

To find religion alive and at the very heart of things for Alexander Hamilton may come somewhat as a surprise for students of contemporary American politics. Yet modern Americans need to appreciate the times in which Hamilton lived; the era involved more than just political upheavals of massive proportions. As historian Douglass Adair has observed, the long period between the seventeenth and nineteenth centuries was "the great watershed in the modern history of religious life and belief."[25] Likewise, the life of Alexander Hamilton was itself a unique watershed of religious life and belief. The man towered as a colossal figure, he swung from moments of triumph to moments of crisis, and he clenched the core meaning that brought discerning purpose to all matters. In all his greatness, however, he was human and he failed. He was sinful and broken—like all human beings. The story of his life, then, is the drama of a man who was both mighty and fallen but who in the end clung ardently to divine grace. May it be the same for the people of his prized United States of America.

---

24. Nott, *A Discourse Delivered*, pp. 20–22.

25. Adair and Harvey, "Was Hamilton a Christian Statesman?" p. 311.

APPENDICES
HAMILTON'S
BIOGRAPHICAL CHRONOLOGY

1757   Born in Charlestown, Nevis, Leeward Islands, British West Indies.

1766   Apprentice clerk in the trading firm of Nicholas Cruger, St. Croix, Virgin Islands.

1772   Landed in Boston, Massachusetts, en route to New York.

1773   Entered King's College, New York.

1774   Published *A Full Vindication of the Measures of Congress from the Calumnies of Their Enemies*.

1775   Published *The Farmer Refuted: or A more impartial and comprehensive View of the Dispute between Great Britain and the Colonies*.

1776   Commissioned a captain in command of the Provincial Company of Artillery. Fought in the battles of Long Island, Harlem Heights, White Plains, and Trenton.

1777   Fought in the Battle of Princeton. Appointed aide-de-camp to General George Washington and promoted to the rank of lieutenant colonel.

1780   Married Elizabeth Schuyler.

1781   Resigned as aide-de-camp to General Washington. Assumed command of New York and Connecticut light infantry battalion. Commanded and led the assault and capture of Redoubt No. 10 at the Battle of Yorktown. Retired from active military duty.

1783   Appointed receiver of taxes for New York. Delegate to Continental Congress. Admitted to practice law in New York.

1784	Opened his first law office on Wall Street, New York. Organizer, Bank of New York.
1785	Associate founder of the New York Society for Promoting the Manumission of Slaves.
1786	New York delegate to Annapolis Convention.
1787	Member of the New York Assembly and delegate to the Constitutional Convention at Philadelphia. Began writing *Federalist* essays.
1788	Reappointed a New York delegate to the Continental Congress. Led ratification efforts for the Constitution in the New York Convention.
1789	Appointed secretary of the treasury for the United States.
1790-94	Published various reports on public credit, a national bank, the U.S. Mint, and manufacturers. Other published writings include: *No Jacobin, Americanus*, the *Tully* letters.
1795	Resigned as secretary of the treasury.
1796	Prepared drafts of President Washington's Farewell Address.
1797	Publicly disclosed his relationship with Mrs. Reynolds.
1798	Appointed inspector-general of the army with the rank of major general.
1800	Retired from the Army.
1801	Founded *New York Evening Post*. Eldest son, Philip Hamilton, killed in a duel.
1802	Proposed the organization of the Christian Constitutional Society.
1804	Died from a mortal wound inflicted in a duel with Aaron Burr.

New York, April, 1802.

Dear Sir,

Your letter of the 12th instant has relieved me from some apprehension. Yet it is well that it should be perfectly understood by the truly sound part of the Federalists, that there do, in fact, exist intrigues in good earnest between several individuals, not unimportant, of the Federal party, and the person in question; which are bottomed upon motives and views by no means auspicious to the real welfare of the country. I am glad to find that it is in contemplation to adopt a plan of conduct. It is very necessary; and, to be useful, it must be efficient and comprehensive in the means which it embraces, at the same time that it must meditate none which are not really constitutional and patriotic. I will comply with your invitation by submitting some ideas, which, from time to time, have passed through my mind. Nothing is more fallacious than to expect to produce any valuable or permanent results, in political projects, by relying merely on the reason of men. Men are rather reasoning than reasonable animals — for the most part governed by the impulse of passion. This is a truth well understood by our adversaries, who have practised upon it with no small benefit to their cause. For at the very moment they are eulogizing the reason of men, and professing to appeal only to that faculty, they are courting the strongest and most active passion of the human heart, Vanity! It is no less true, that the

Fede.

Hamilton's 1802 letter, to James A. Bayard, proposing the formation of a Christian Constitutional Society.

Hamilton's Proposal for the Christian Constitutional Society

To James A. Bayard

New-York April [16–21] 1802

Dear Sir,

Your letter of the 12th inst. Has relieved me from some apprehension. Yet it is well that it should be perfectly understood by the truly sound part of the Fœderalists, that there do in fact exist intrigues in good earnest, between several individuals not unimportant, of the Fœderal Party, and the person in question; which are bottomed upon motives & views, by no means auspicious to the real welfare of the country. I am glad to find that it is in contemplation to adopt a plan of conduct. It is very necessary; & to be useful it must be efficient & comprehensive in the means which it embraces, at the same time that it must meditate none which are not really constitutional & patriotic. I will comply with your invitation by submitting some ideas which from time to time have passed through my mind. Nothing is more fallacious than to expect to produce any valuable or permanent results, in political projects, by relying merely on the reason of men. Men are rather reasoning tha[n] reasonable animals for the most part governed by the impulse of passion. This is a truth well understood by our adversaries who have practised upon it with no small benefit to their cause. For at the very moment they are eulogizing the reason of men & professing to appeal only to that faculty, they are courting the strongest & most active passions of the human heart—VANITY!

It is no less true that the Fœderalists seem not to have attended to the fact sufficiently; and that they erred in relying so much on the rectitude & utility of their measures, as to have neglected the cultivation of popular favour by fair & justifiable expedients. The observation has been repeatedly

Source: *Hamilton Papers*, 25:605–610.

made by me to individuals with whom I particularly conversed & expedients suggested for gaining good will which were never adopted. Unluckily however for us in the competition for the passions of the people our opponents have great advantages over us; for the plain reason, that the vicious are far more active than the good passions, and that to win the latter to our side we must renounce our principles & our objects, & unite in corrupting public opinion till it becomes fit for nothing but mischief. Yet unless we can contrive to take hold of & carry along with us some strong feelings of the mind we shall in vain calculate upon any substantial or durable results. Whatever plan we may adopt, to be successful must be founded on the truth of this proposition. And perhaps it is not very easy for us to give it full effect; especially not without some deviations, we must consider whether it be possible for us to succeed without in some degree employing the weapons which have been employed against us, & whether the actual state and future prospect of things, be not such as to justify the reciprocal use of them. I need not tell you that I do not mean to countenance the imitation of things intrinsically unworthy, but only of such as may be denominated irregular, such as in a sound & stable order of things ought not to exist. Neither are you to infer that any revolutionary result is contemplated. In my opinion the present Constitution is the standard to which we are to cling. Under its banners, bona fide must we combat our political foes—rejecting all changes but through the channel itself provides for amendments. By these general views of the subject have my reflections been guided. I now offer you the outline of the plan which they have suggested. Let an Association be formed to be denominated, "The Christian Constitutional Society." Its objects to be

1st   The support of the Christian Religion.

2nd   The support of the Constitution of the United States.

Its Organization.

1st   A directing council consisting of a President & 12 Members, of whom 4 & the President to be a quorum.

2nd   A sub-directing council in each State consisting of a Vice-President & 12 Members, of whom 4 with the Vice-President to be a quorum &

3rd   As many societies in each State, as local circumstances may permit to be formed by the Sub-directing council.

The Meeting at Washington to Nominate the *President & Vice-President* together with *4 Members of each* of the councils, who are to complete their own numbers respectively.

Its Means.

1st   The diffusion of information. For this purpose not only the Newspapers but pamphlets must be la[r]gely employed & to do this a fund must be created. 5 dollars annually for 8 years, to be contributed by each member who can readily afford it, (taking care not to burden the less able brethren) may afford a competent fund for a competent time. It is essential to be able to disseminate *gratis* useful publications. Whenever it can be done, & there is a press, clubs should be formed to meet once a week, read the newspapers & prepare essays paragraphs & etc.

2nd   The use of all lawful means in concert to promote the election of *fit men.* A lively correspondence must be kept up between the different Societies.

3rd   The promoting of instructions of a charitable & useful nature in the management of the Fœderalists. The populous cities ought to be particularly attended to. Perhaps it will be well to institute in such places 1st Societies for the relief of Emigrants—2nd Academies each with one professor for instructing different Classes of Mechanics & Elements of Chemistry. The cities have been employed by the Jacobins to give an impulse to the country. And it is believed to be an alarming fact, that while the question of Presidential Election was pending in the House of Rs. Parties were organized in several of the Cities, in the event of there being no election, to cut off the leading Fœderalists & seize the Government. An Act of association to be drawn up in concise general terms. It need only designate the "name" "objects" & contain an engagement to promote the objects by all lawful means, and particularly by the diffusion of Information. This act to be signed by every member.

The foregoing to be the principle Engine. In addition let measures be adopted to bring as soon as possible the repeal of the Judiciary law before the Supreme Court. Afterwards, if not before, let as many Legislatures as can be prevailed upon, instruct their Senators to endeavour to procure a repeal of the repealing law. The body of New-England speaking the same language will give a powerful impulse. In Congress our friends to *propose* little, to agree candidly to all good measures, & to resist & expose all bad. This is a general sketch of what has occurred to me. It is at the service of my friends for so much as it may be worth. With true esteem & regard

    Dr Sir   Yours   AH

Hamilton's Last Moments Recounted by Benjamin Moore

Rt. Rev. Benjamin Moore to William Coleman

[New York] Thursday evening, July 12.

Mr. Coleman,

The public mind being extremely agitated by the melancholy fate of that great man, ALEXANDER HAMILTON, I have thought it would be grateful to my fellow-citizens, would provide against misrepresentation, and perhaps, be conducive to the advancement of the cause of Religion, were I to give a narrative of some facts which have fallen under my own observation, during the time which elapsed between the fatal duel and his departure out of this world.

Yesterday morning, immediately after he was brought from Hoboken to the house of Mr. Bayard, at Greenwich, a message was sent informing me of the sad event, accompanied by a request from General Hamilton, that I would come to him for the purpose of administering the holy communion. I went; but being desirous to afford time for serious reflection, and conceiving that under existing circumstances, it would be right and proper to avoid every appearance of precipitancy in performing one of the most solemn offices of our religion, I did not then comply with his desire. At one o'clock I was again called on to visit him. Upon my entering the room and approaching his bed, with the utmost calmness and composure he said, "My dear Sir, you perceive my unfortunate situation, and no doubt have been made acquainted with the circumstances which led to it. It is my desire to receive the Communion at your hands. I hope you will not conceive there is any impropriety in my request." He added, "It has for some time past been the wish of my heart, and it was my intention to take

Source: Syrett and Cooke, *Interview in Weehawken*, pp. 144–147.

an early opportunity of uniting myself to the church, by the reception of that holy ordinance." I observed to him, that he must be very sensible of the delicate and trying situation in which I was then placed; that however desirous I might be to afford consolation to a fellow mortal in distress; still, it was my duty as a minister of the gospel, to hold up the law of God as paramount to all other law; and that, therefore, under the influence of such sentiments, I must unequivocally condemn the practice which had brought him to his present unhappy condition. He acknowledged the propriety of these sentiments, and declared that he viewed the late transaction with sorrow and contrition. I then asked him, "Should it please God, to restore you to health, Sir, will you never be again engaged in a similar transaction? and will you employ all your influence in society to discountenance this barbarous custom?" His answer was, "That, Sir, is my deliberate intention."

I proceeded to converse with him on the subject of his receiving the Communion; and told him that with respect to the qualifications of those who wished to become partakers of that holy ordinance, my enquiries could not be made in language more expressive than that which was used by our Church. "Do you sincerely repent of your sins past? Have you a lively faith in God's mercy through Christ, with a thankful remembrance of the death of Christ? And are you disposed to live in love and charity with all men?" He lifted up his hands and said, "With the utmost sincerity of heart I can answer those questions in the affirmative—I have no ill will against Col. Burr. I met him with a fixed resolution to do him no harm—I forgive all that happened." I then observed to him, that the terrors of the divine law were to be announced to the obdurate and impenitent: but that the consolations of the Gospel were to be offered to the humble and contrite heart: that I had no reason to doubt his sincerity, and would proceed immediately to gratify his wishes. The communion was then administered, which he received with great devotion, and his heart afterwards appeared to be perfectly at rest. I saw him again this morning, when, with his last faultering words, he expressed a strong confidence in the mercy of God through the intercession of the Redeemer. I remained with him until 2 o'clock this afternoon, when death closed the awful scene—he expired without a struggle, and almost without a groan.

By reflecting on this melancholy event, let the humble believer be encouraged ever to hold fast that precious faith which is the only source of true consolation in the last extremity of nature. Let the Infidel be persuaded true consolation in the last extremity of nature. Let the Infidel be persuaded to abandon his opposition to that gospel which the strong, inquisitive, and comprehensive mind of a HAMILTON embraced, in his last moments, as the truth from heaven. Let those who are disposed to justify the practice of duelling, be induced, by this simple narrative, to view with abhorrence that custom which has occasioned an irreparable loss to a worthy and most afflicted family; which has deprived his friends of a beloved companion, his profession of one of its brightest ornaments, and his country of a great statesman and a real patriot.

> With great respect,
> I remain your friend and servant,
>
> BENJAMIN MOORE

HAMILTON'S LAST MOMENTS RECOUNTED BY JOHN M. MASON

Rev. Dr. John M. Mason to the Editor of the Commercial Advertiser

Sir,

HAVING read, in your paper of the 16th, a very imperfect account of my conversation with General Hamilton, the day previous to his decease, I judge it my duty to lay the following narrative before the public.

On the morning of Wednesday the 11th instant, shortly after the rumour of the General's injury had created an alarm in the city, a note from Dr. Post informed me that "he was extremely ill at Mr. William Bayard's, and expressed a particular desire to see me as soon as possible." I went immediately. The exchange of melancholy salutation, on entering the General's apartment, was succeeded by a silence which he broke by saying, that he "had been anxious to see me, and have the sacrament administered to him; and that this was still his wish." I replied, that "it gave me unutterable pain to receive from him any request to which I could not accede: that, in the present stance, a compliance was incompatible with all my obligations, as it is a principle in our churches never to administer the Lord's Supper privately to any person under any circumstances." He urged me no further. I then remarked to him, that, "the Holy Communion is an exhibition and pledge of the mercies which the Son of God has purchased; that the absence of the sign does not exclude from the merices signified; which were accessible to him by faith in their gracious Author." "I am aware," said he, "of that. It was only as a sign that I wanted it." A short pause ensued. I resumed the discourse, by observing that "I had nothing to address to him in his affliction, but that the same *gospel of the grace of God*, which it is my office to preach to the most obscure and illiterate: that in the sight of God all men are on a level, as *all have sinned, and come short of his glory*; and they must apply to him for pardon and life, as sinners, whose only refuge is in his *grace reigning by righteousness through our Lord Jesus*

Source: Mason, *An Oration Commemorative*, pp. 33–38.

Christ." "I perceive it to be so," said he; "I am a sinner: I look to his mercy." I then averted to "the infinite merit of the Redeemer, as the *propitiation for sin*, the sole ground of our acceptance with God; the sole channel of his favour to us; and cited the following passages of scripture:—*There is no other name given under heaven among men, whereby we must be saved, but the name of Jesus. He is able to save them to the uttermost who come unto God by him, seeing he ever liveth to make intercession for them. The blood of Jesus Christ cleanseth from all sin.*" This last passage introduced the affair of the duel, on which I reminded the General, that he was not to be instructed as to its moral aspect, that *the precious blood of Christ* was as effectual and as necessary to wash away the transgression which had involved him in suffering, as any other transgression; and that he must there, and there alone, seek peace for his conscience, and a hope that should "*not make him ashamed.*" He assented, with strong emotion, to these representations, and declared his abhorrence of the whole transaction. "It was always," added he, "against my principles. I used every expedient to avoid the interview; but I have found, for some time past, that my life *must* be exposed to that man. I went to the field determined not to take his life." He repeated his disavowal of all intention to hurt Mr. Burr; the anguish of his mind in recollecting what had passed; and his humble hope of forgiveness from his God. I recurred to the topic of the divine compassions; the freedom of pardon in the Redeemer Jesus to perishing sinners. "That grace, my dear General, which brings salvation, is rich"—"Yes," interrupted he, "it is *rich grace*." "And on that grace," continued I, "a sinner has the highest encouragement to repose his confidence, because it is tendered to him upon the surest foundation; the scripture testifying that *we have redemption through the blood of Jesus, the forgiveness of sins according to the riches of his grace.*" Here the General, letting go my hand, which he had held from the moment I sat down at his bed-side, clasped his hands together, and, looking up towards heaven, said, with emphasis, "I have a tender reliance on the mercy of the Almighty, through the merits of the Lord Jesus Christ." He replaced his hand in mine, and appearing somewhat spent, closed his eyes. A little after, he fastened them on me, and I proceeded. "The simple truths of the Gospel, my dear Sir, which require no abstruse investigation, but faith in the veracity of God who cannot lie, are best suited to your present condition, and they are full of consolation." "I feel them to be so," replied he. I then repeated these texts of scripture:—*It is a faithful saying, and worthy of all acceptation, that Christ Jesus came into the world to save sinners, and of sinners the Chief. I, even I, am he that blotteth out thy transgressions for mine own sake, and will not remember thy sins. Come now, and let us reason together, saith the Lord; though your sins be as scarlet, they shall be white as snow, though they be red like crimson, they shall be as wool.* "This," said he, "is my support. Pray for me." "Shall I pray with you?" "Yes." I prayed with him, and heard him whisper as I went along; which I supposed to be his concurrence with the petitions. As the conclusion he said "Amen. God grant it."

Being about to part with him, I told him "I had one request to make." He asked "what it was?" I answered, "that whatever might be the issue of his affliction, he would give his testimony against the practice of duelling." "I will," said he, "I have done it. If that," evidently anticipating the event, "if it be the issue, you will find it in writing. If it please God that I recover, I shall do it in a manner that will effectually put me out of its reach in future." I mentioned, once more, the importance of renouncing every other dependence for the eternal world, but the mercy of God in Christ Jesus; with a particular reference to the catastrophe of the morning. The General was affected, and said, "Let us not pursue the subject any further, it agitates me." He laid his hands upon my breast, with symptoms of uneasiness, which indicated an increased difficulty of speaking. I then took my leave. He pressed my hand affectionately, and desired to see me again at a proper interval. As I was retiring, he lifted up his hands in the attitude of prayer, and said feebly, "God be merciful to -------." His voice sunk, so that I heard not the rest distinctly, but understood him to quote the world of the publican in the gospel, and to end the sentence with, "me a sinner."

I saw him, a second time, on the morning of Thursday; but from his appearance, and what I had heard, supposing that he could not speak without severe effort, I had no conversation with him. I prayed for a moment at his bed side in company with his overwhelmed family and friends; and for the rest, was one of the mourning spectators of his composure and dignity in suffering. His mind remained in its former state: and he viewed with calmness his approaching dissolution. I left him between twelve and one, and at two, as the public know, he breathed his last.

I am Sir,

With much respect,
Your obedient servant,

J. M. Mason

New-York, July 18, 1804

Alexander Hamilton

Selected Bibliography

Bailey, Ralph Edward. *An American Colossus: The Singular Career of Alexander Hamilton*. Boston: Lothrop, Lee & Shephard, 1933.

Bowers, Claude G. *Jefferson and Hamilton: The Struggle for Democracy in America*. Boston and New York: Houghton Mifflin, 1925.

Brookhiser, Richard. *Alexander Hamilton, America*. New York: The Free Press, 1999.

Fleming, Thomas. *Duel: Alexander Hamilton, Aaron Burr and the Future of America*. New York: Basic Books, 1999.

Hendrickson, Robert. *Hamilton II*. New York: Mason Charter, 1976.

_____. *The Rise and Fall of Alexander Hamilton*. New York: Van Nostrand Reinhold, 1981.

Humes, James C. *My Fellow Americans*. New York: Praeger, 1992.

Johnson, F. Ernest, ed. *Wellsprings of the American Spirit*. New York: Cooper Square Publishers, 1964.

Kline, Mary-Jo, ed. *Alexander Hamilton: A Biography in His Own Words*. New York: Newsweek, 1973.

McDonald, Forrest. *Alexander Hamilton: A Bibliography*. New York: W. W. Norton, 1979.

Morris, Richard B., ed. *Alexander Hamilton and the Founding of the Nation*. New York: The Dial Press, 1957.

Morris, Richard B. *Witnesses at the Creation: Hamilton, Madison, Jay, and the Constitution*. New York: Holt, Rineheart and Winston, 1985.

Syrett, Harold C., ed. *The Papers of Alexander Hamilton*. 25 vols. New York: Columbia University Press, 1961–77.

Vandenberg, Arthur Hendrick. *The Greatest American: Alexander Hamilton*. New York: G. P. Putnam's Sons, 1921.

ABOUT THE AUTHOR

Christopher S. Yates, a Witherspoon Fellow at the Family Research Council in the fall of 1999, received his bachelor of arts in American history from the University of North Carolina in 1998.

The Witherspoon Fellowship is the civic and cultural leadership development program of the Family Research Council. Its mission is to inspire a transcendent vision for the calling and obligations of citizenship and to foster Christian worldview reflection and principled action on behalf of the family for the betterment of civil society and good government. In addition to sponsoring public lectures, symposia, colloquia, and publications, the Fellowship hosts a resident internship program devoted to the intellectual, professional, and spiritual formation of college students.

Founded in 1983, the Family Research Council is a nonprofit research and educational organization dedicated to articulating and advancing a family-centered philosophy of public life. In addition to providing policy research and analysis for the legislative, executive, and judicial branches of the federal government, the Council seeks to inform news media, the academic community, business and religious leaders, and the general public about family issues that affect the nation.

The Family Research Council relies solely on the generosity of individuals, families, foundations, and businesses for financial support. The Internal Revenue Service recognizes the Council as a tax-exempt, 501(c)(3) charitable organization. Donations to the Council are therefore tax-deductible in accordance with section 170 of the Internal Revenue Code.

Located at 801 G Street, N.W., Washington, D.C., the headquarters of the Family Research Council provides its staff with strategic access to government decision-making centers, national media offices, and information sources. Owned by Faith, Family, and Freedom, L.L.C., the six-story office building was completed in 1996 through the generosity of the Edgar Prince and Richard DeVos families of western Michigan. Visitors are welcome during normal business hours. Please call (202) 393-2100 in advance to ensure a pleasant and productive visit.

FAMILY RESEARCH COUNCIL
801 G Street, N.W.
Washington, DC 20001
(800)225-4008
www.frc.org

THE *Witherspoon* FELLOWSHIP

The *Witherspoon* Fellowship is the civic and cultural leadership development program of the Family Research Council. Its mission is to inspire a transcendent vision for the calling and obligations of citizenship and to foster Christian worldview reflection and principled action on behalf of the family for the betterment of civil society and good government. In addition to sponsoring public lectures, symposia, colloquia, and publications, the Fellowship hosts a resident internship program devoted to the intellectual, professional, and spiritual formation of college students.

Founded in 1983, the Family Research Council is a nonprofit research and educational organization dedicated to articulating and advancing a family-centered philosophy of public life. In addition to providing policy research and analysis for the legislative, executive, and judicial branches of the federal government, the Council seeks to inform news media, the academic community, business and religious leaders, and the general public about family issues that affect the nation.

The Family Research Council relies solely on the generosity of individuals, families, foundations, and businesses for financial support. The Internal Revenue Service recognizes the Council as a tax-exempt, 501(c)(3) charitable organization. Donations to the Council are therefore tax-deductible in accordance with section 170 of the Internal Revenue Code.

Located at 801 G Street, N.W., Washington, D.C., the headquarters of the Family Research Council provides its staff with strategic access to government decision-making centers, national media offices, and information sources. Owned by Faith, Family, and Freedom, LLC, the six-story office building was completed in 1996 through the generosity of the Edgar Prince and Richard DeVos families of western Michigan. Visitors are welcome during normal business hours. Please call (202) 393-2100 in advance to ensure a pleasant and productive visit.

FAMILY RESEARCH COUNCIL
801 G Street, N.W.
Washington, DC 20001
(800)225-4008
www.frc.org